# MULTICULTURAL
# STORYTIME
# MAGIC

ALA Editions purchases fund advocacy,
awareness, and accreditation programs
for library professionals worldwide.

# MULTICULTURAL STORYTIME MAGIC

Kathy MacMillan
and
Christine Kirker

AMERICAN LIBRARY ASSOCIATION

Chicago   2012

**KATHY MACMILLAN** is a writer, American Sign Language interpreter, librarian, and storyteller. She is the author of *Try Your Hand at This! Easy Ways to Incorporate Sign Language into Your Programs* (Scarecrow Press, 2005) and *A Box Full of Tales* (American Library Association, 2008), and the coauthor of *Storytime Magic* (American Library Association, 2009) and *Kindergarten Magic* (American Library Association, 2012). She holds an MLS from the University of Maryland, and her library career includes work at the Maryland School for the Deaf and the Carroll County (Maryland) Public Library. Kathy presents storytelling programs introducing sign language through Stories by Hand (www.storiesbyhand.com), and trainings and resources for enhancing storytimes through www.storytimestuff.net.

**CHRISTINE KIRKER** is a Children's Library Associate with the Carroll County (Maryland) Public Library. Since joining the library staff in 2005, Christine has developed and presented many programs for children of all ages and is the coauthor of *Storytime Magic* (American Library Association, 2009) and *Kindergarten Magic* (American Library Association, 2012). Previously, Christine spent ten years at the University of Maryland, Baltimore County (UMBC), as a research analyst for the Office of Institutional Research. She graduated from UMBC in 1992. Christine presents trainings and programs introducing ways to enhance storytimes through www.storytimestuff.net.

---

Illustrations by Melanie Fitz and Christine Kirker

The American Sign Language (ASL) graphic images in this book can be found in *American Sign Language Clip and Create 5,* a software product of the Institute for Disabilities Research and Training (IDRT), and are used here with the permission of the publisher. To purchase a copy or learn more about IDRT's other ASL-accessible software, visit www.idrt.com.

Printed in the United States of America

16   15   14   13   12      5   4   3   2   1

While extensive effort has gone into ensuring the reliability of the information in this book, the publisher makes no warranty, express or implied, with respect to the material contained herein. We have made every effort to provide accurate pronunciation guides for the foreign language materials in this book; we acknowledge, however, that pronunciations by native users may vary due to the dynamic nature of language across settings and regions.

ISBNs: 978-0-8389-1142-6 (paper); 978-0-8389-9467-2 (PDF). For more information on digital formats, visit the ALA Store at alastore.ala.org and select eEditions.

**Library of Congress Cataloging-in-Publication Data**
MacMillan, Kathy, 1975–
    Multicultural storytime magic / Kathy MacMillan and Christine Kirker.
      pages   cm
    Includes bibliographical references and indexes.
    ISBN 978-0-8389-1142-6
    1. Children's libraries—Activity programs—United States. 2. Multicultural education—Activity programs—United States. 3. Storytelling—United States. I. Kirker, Christine. II. Title.
    Z718.3.M2525 2012
    027.62'51—dc23                      2011043434

Book design by Karen Sheets de Gracia in Candy Randy, Kristen ITC, Georgia, and Helvetica
Composition by Dianne M. Rooney

♾ This paper meets the requirements of ANSI/NISO Z39.48–1992 (Permanence of Paper).

*For my library mentors, Micki Freeny and Jackie Sollers.
See what you started?*

—KM


*For my family, who allow me to unleash my sillies!*

—CMK

# Contents

**WEB** Flannelboard patterns, craft patterns, and worksheets are available online at alaeditions.org/webextras.

# Acknowledgments

**WE WOULD** first like to thank Melanie Fitz for her beautiful illustrations. Melanie, thank you for sharing your talent with us and our readers.

Gracias, spasiba, and dziękuję to Ashleigh Kirker, Janet Henry, Jennie Levine, Patrick Stewart, and Liz Lipinski, who assisted with translations and pronunciation guides.

Thank you once again to Corinne Vinopol and the Institute for Disabilities Research and Training Inc. for their continued support and dedication to sharing American Sign Language with the library community.

Thank you to the amazing production staff at ALA Editions, whose beautiful book designs always wow us.

Thank you to the many librarians, past and present, who opened and continue to open up the world to the young people they serve.

# Introduction

**CONSIDER THE FOLLOWING:**

- By the year 2050, the number of Asians in the United States is expected to reach 22.7 million, an increase of 213 percent over census figures from the year 2000 (Shresta 2006, 19).

- In the 2000 U.S. census, 12.6 percent of the U.S. population identified themselves as Hispanic. This number is projected to rise to 24.4 percent by 2050 (Shresta 2006, 21–22).

- Since the passage of the Education for All Handicapped Children Act in 1975 (reauthorized as the Individuals with Disabilities Education Act in 1990 and 2004), a great many deaf children have been educated in public schools, leading to a greater number of hearing children being exposed to American Sign Language (ASL; Safford 2004). Though estimates vary due to inconsistent record keeping, ASL is commonly held to be the third or fourth most-used language in the United States.

- With increasing access to technologies that link us to others around the world, today's children will grow up more connected than ever before to their counterparts in other countries.

As these facts illustrate, our society is growing more diverse by the day. Storytime audiences reflect that diversity, and so it is more important than ever that the materials used in programs reflect the many colors of our world. Yet too often *multiculturalism* means offering special once-a-year programs surrounding particular holidays. In this book, we offer a new paradigm for multicultural programs, one in which diversity is woven into every storytime, no matter the topic.

Here you will find concrete book recommendations, fingerplays, flannelboards, and other activities that can be incorporated into everyday programs. Arranged thematically around forty-four popular storytime subjects, these original and traditional resources from all over the world will enrich storytimes for ages 2 and up. Materials especially appropriate for 2- and 3-year-olds are marked with an asterisk (*). You can print full-sized versions of all the illustrations, flannelboards, and worksheets from the Multicultural Storytime Magic Web Extra page at www.alaeditions.org/webextras/.

## What Is Cultural Diversity?

Cultural diversity in storytimes is more than just throwing in a story from another country—it's a mind-set that says that children deserve to be exposed to a wide variety of cultures and experiences. It's not a once-a-year thing; it's an everyday occurrence. We must convey to children not only an attitude of respect for the diversity of cultures around the world but also an understanding of the plurality of cultures and abilities represented in our own country and in our own neighborhoods.

It is an awesome responsibility; after all, as Janice N. Harrington, author of *Multiculturalism in Library Programming for Children*, points out, "Librarians' decisions produce and control the cultural images that children experience in the library" (1994, 3).

The activities in this book offer concrete, hands-on ways for young children to explore diversity. We hope that you will find the suggestions here a springboard and that these activities will inspire you to bring elements of multiculturalism into every program you present, no matter what the topic. It all begins with awareness of diversity and a willingness to seek out a variety of resources.

In this book, you'll find resources relating to

- Diversity in American society: materials showing Americans of all backgrounds
- Diversity in the world: traditional and modern materials from many lands
- Diversity of abilities: materials showing people with various disabilities and members of Deaf culture

For additional exciting storytime resources, visit the authors' website at www.storytimestuff.net, and be sure to sign up for our free seasonal newsletter to receive exclusive storytime resources right in your inbox.

## Works Cited

Harrington, Janice N. 1994. *Multiculturalism in Library Programming for Children*. Chicago: American Library Association.

Safford, Philip Lane. 2004. "Special Education." In *Encyclopedia of Children and Childhood in History and Society*, edited by Paula S. Fass. New York: Macmillan Reference USA. Available at www.faqs.org/childhood/So-Th/Special-Education.html.

Shresta, Laura B. 2006. *The Changing Demographic Profile of the United States*. Congressional Report. Washington, DC: Library of Congress.

# 1

# ABC Time

## Books

**1** *Handsigns: A Sign Language Alphabet* **by Kathleen Fain. San Francisco: Chronicle, 1993.**

This book presents an alphabet of animals, accompanied by the ASL manual alphabet.

**2** ***ABC for You and Me* by Meg Girnis. Morton Grove, IL: Whitman, 2000.**

In many ways this is a standard alphabet book, with each page featuring a letter alongside a word and an object that begin with that letter. What's notable is the diversity of the children in the colorful photos, including many children with Down syndrome. By providing images of kids with Down syndrome in an everyday context instead of a "disability" context, this book presents a powerful message of inclusion.

**3** *Japan ABCs* **by Sarah Heiman. Minneapolis, MN: Picture Window Books, 2003.**

This book provides an overview of the people, places, and customs of Japan while working through the English alphabet. After reading, ask the children if they recognize anything in the book that we have here in America. Examples could be chopsticks or cherry blossom festivals, which are similar to the Hanami celebration. Ask if anyone has eaten any of the foods described in the book, and have the children choose the most interesting things in the book.

**4** *¡Marimba!* **by Pat Mora. New York: Clarion, 2006.**

Once a year a monkey sings the zookeepers to sleep. Then he plays his marimba and all the *animales* wake! An alphabet of animals combines with music and dance in this playful book. The text uses both the English and Spanish animal names. Use the glossary in the back for translation and pronunciation help.

# Flannelboard

## 5 *ABC × 3* by Marthe Jocelyn. Toronto, ON: Tundra Books, 2005.

With bold lines and bright colors, this simple ABC book presents a picture for each letter of the alphabet, along with text in English, Spanish, and French.

Pass out the pictures. As you call out the letters, the children should place the appropriate items on the flannelboard. Discuss how the words in different languages are often similar or sometimes exactly the same.

# Fingerplays and Songs

### 6  *Letters Around the World (to the tune of "Frère Jacques")

Before singing this song, explain that, although many languages use the same alphabet that English uses, the letters are pronounced differently in some languages. This song will show an example of that difference.

When I sing the alphabet, it's
ABC, ABC.
I can sing my letters, I know all my letters
ABC, ABC.

But in French when we say the alphabet, it's
ABC (ah, bay, say), ABC (ah, bay, say).
I can sing my letters, I know all my letters
ABC, ABC.

### 7  *ABC Rhyme Time

Maracas are traditional percussion instruments used throughout the Caribbean and Latin America. Inexpensive maracas can be purchased in bulk for storytime use from many school and library supply companies.

Use a maraca to draw each letter in the air, speaking the letter and shaking the maraca as you go. Make sure you shape each letter slowly so that the children can follow. This activity develops gross motor skills, letter knowledge, and rhythmic sense and supports kinesthetic learning.

Shake your maracas A to Z.
Shake out the alphabet with me!

### 8  Signing ABCs (to the tune of "The Alphabet Song")

Teach the ASL manual alphabet as you sing this song.

You can sing your ABCs
With your voice quick as you please.
Can you sing it with your hands?
Come on now, give it a chance.
Come and learn to sign with me.
We will *sign* our ABCs.
   A B C D E F G
   H I J K L M N O P
   Q R S
   T U V
   W X Y and Z
Now we've signed our ABCs.
Show your favorite letter to me!

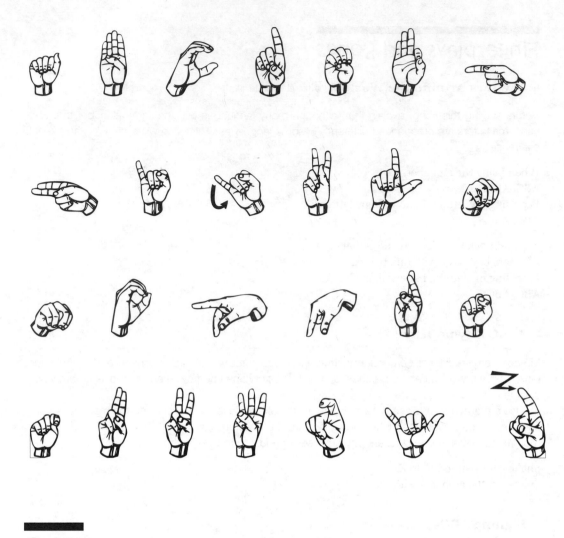

## Craft

### 9 A Multicultural Alphabet

*Materials:* alphabet coloring sheet (from website), crayons, glue

*Directions:* Color as desired.

**A**
Alps

**B**
burrito

**C**
chopsticks

**D**
didgeridoo

**E**
Eiffel Tower

**F**
falafel

**G**
Great Wall of China

**H**
hockey

**I**
igloo

**J**
jambalaya

**K**
kung fu

**L**
Leaning Tower
of Pisa

**M**
maracas

**N**
Nile River

**O**
obi

**P**
pagoda

**Q**
quetzal

**R**
rice ball

**S**
sari

**T**
tepee

**U**
ukelele

**V**
Valkyrie

**W**
wooden shoes

**X**
X (Roman
numeral 10)

**Y**
yoga

**Z**
Zen garden

From *Multicultural Storytime Magic* by Kathy MacMillan and Christine Kirker

# 2

# Bath Time

## Books

**10** ***Maisy Takes a Bath* by Lucy Cousins. Cambridge, MA: Candlewick, 2002.**

It's Maisy's bath time, but Tallulah wants to play. This toddler-friendly book is brief and colorful. Make it multicultural by incorporating Spanish or ASL vocabulary as you read.

*Spanish vocabulary:*

bath: *el baño* (el BAHN-yo)  bubble: *la burbuja* (la boor-BOO-ha)
duck: *el pato* (el PAH-toe)  play: *jugar* (hoo-GAR)

*ASL vocabulary:*

**11** ***The Way We Do It in Japan*** **by Geneva Cobb Iijima. Park Ridge, IL: Whitman, 2002.**

Gregory learns a new way of life when his father's company sends the family to Japan. After reading, discuss the differences between the way people live in America and Japan. Some areas to explore are eating, sleeping arrangements, bathing, and school.

**12** ***Ruler of the Courtyard*** **by Rukhsana Khan. New York: Penguin, 2003.**

Saba, a young Pakistani girl, meets chickens and a snake on her trip to the bathhouse. After reading the story, ask the children to name the similarities and differences they noticed between where and how they bathe and how Saba bathes.

# Flannelboard

## 13 *Carlos and the Squash Plant

Adapted from the book by Jan Romero Stevens (Flagstaff, AZ: Northland, 1993).

Carlos lived on a farm in the mountains of New Mexico. His parents were farmers and tended a garden plot next to their adobe home. They grew many wonderful vegetables, but Carlos's favorite was squash because he loved when his mother made spicy *calabacitas* (call-ah-bah-SEE-tahs).

Carlos worked very hard in the garden and often came home with dirt everywhere—under his fingernails, between his toes, and even inside his ears. But Carlos hated taking baths! (*Ask children, "Who here likes taking baths?"*) Well, every day his mother would warn him, "If you don't wash your ears, a squash plant will grow in them!" But Carlos did not believe her.

One evening, Carlos's mother called him in to take a bath before dinner. Carlos went into the bathroom and wiped off his face with a washcloth, but he did not take a bath. Then he had dinner and went to bed.

The next morning, Carlos's ear felt itchy. When he looked in the mirror he saw a small green stem with two leaves growing in his right ear. Carlos quickly grabbed a wide-brimmed hat to cover the plant so his mother would not see it at breakfast, and then he ran outside to work in the garden.

Again that evening, Carlos's mother called him in to take a bath before dinner. Carlos went into the bathroom and wiped off his face with a washcloth, but he did not take a bath. Then he had dinner and went to bed.

The next morning, Carlos woke to find the green plant was bigger than before! Now there were five leaves. Carlos quickly grabbed a wide-brimmed hat to cover the plant so his mother would not see it at breakfast, and then he ran outside to work in the garden.

Again that evening, Carlos's mother called him in to take a bath before dinner. Carlos went into the bathroom and wiped off his face with a washcloth, but he did not take a bath. Then he had dinner and went to bed.

When Carlos woke up the next morning, his head felt very heavy. A long green vine with yellow blossoms hung down the pillow and trailed onto the floor. Carlos pulled and tugged on the vine, but it wouldn't come out. Carlos ran to his father's closet and found an even larger hat. He coiled the vine on top of his head and put the hat over it. Carlos grabbed breakfast from the kitchen and ran outside to eat.

That day, the weather was very breezy, but Carlos was careful to hold on to his hat. He let go for just a moment to wipe his face, when his mother called him in for dinner. Panicking, Carlos covered his head with his arms and ran to take a bath before his mother could even tell him to. This time, Carlos filled the tub with water and began scrubbing his ears. Amazingly, the squash plant began to shrink. The more he scrubbed, the smaller it became, until finally, the vine had completely disappeared.

That night, Carlos went to dinner without a hat and proudly announced that he had taken a bath and had remembered to wash his ears.

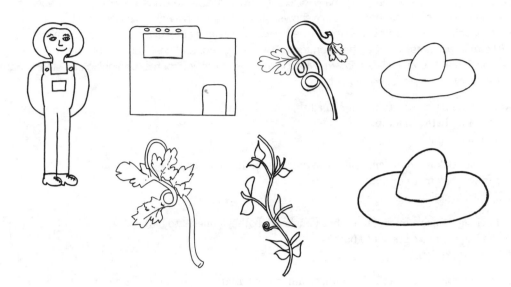

# Fingerplays and Songs

### 14  Clean or Dirty

Teach the children the Italian words below, then say each sentence, pausing at the end of each line to allow the children to supply the correct word.

*Italian vocabulary:*

>   clean: *pulito* (POO-lee-toe)
>   dirty: *sporco* (SPORK-oh)

I woke up this morning and brushed my teeth, and now my teeth are . . . (*pulito*)!

I got dressed and went to school, but along the way I stepped in a mud puddle, and now my shoes are . . . (*sporco*)!

At school our teacher told us to tidy our desks, so I recycled my old papers. Now my desk is . . . (*pulito*)!

Then it was time for art class. We got to finger paint today! Now my hands and my smock are . . . (*sporco*)!

Then it was time for lunch. I washed my hands, and now they are . . . (*pulito*)!

We had chocolate ice cream for dessert. It melted all over my face, so now my face is . . . (*sporco*)!

I washed the ice cream off my face and hands, and now they are . . . (*pulito*)!

Then we had recess and I played in the sandbox. Now I am . . . (*sporco*)!

When school was over I went home, and Mommy said, "You need to take a bath." So I did. Now I am . . . (*pulito*)!

**15 Splish, Splash, Splish!** (to the tune of "Here We Go 'Round the Mulberry Bush")

People around the world bathe in many different ways. Most Americans take baths or showers. In Japan, people often clean themselves in a shower stall, then soak in a hot tub called an *onsen*. In African villages, people wash themselves without wasting water. Villagers often use a bucket of warm water and a plastic mug or container. They dampen themselves, soap up, and rinse, using only the water in one bucket. In Turkey, people use a *hamam,* which is a series of bathing rooms, beginning in a steam room and eventually ending in a cool water bath.

In America we bathe in a tub, bathe in a tub, bathe in a tub,
In America we bathe in a tub,
Splish, splash, splish!

In Japan we soak in an *onsen*, soak in an *onsen*, soak in an *onsen*,
In Japan we soak in an *onsen*,
Splish, splash, splish!

African villagers use a bucket to bathe, a bucket to bathe, a bucket to bathe,
African villagers use a bucket to bathe,
Splish, splash, splish!

In Turkey people steam in the *hamam*, steam in the *hamam*, steam in the *hamam*,
In Turkey people steam in the *hamam*,
Splish, splash, splish!

All over the world people wash themselves, people wash themselves, people wash themselves,
All over the world people wash themselves,
Splish, splash, splish!

**16 *"Look at My Hands"** from *Signing Time Songs*, volumes 1–3 by Rachel de Azevedo Coleman. Salt Lake City, UT: Two Little Hands, 2002.**

Teach the signs DIRTY and CLEAN and use them as you sing this song.

# Craft

### 17  We All Take Baths

*Materials:* bath time coloring sheet (from website), crayons

*Directions:*

1. Discuss the pictures of the children on the coloring sheet and how people bathe in different ways around the world.
2. Color the picture as desired.

# 3

# Bedtime

## Books

**18**  ***Hush! A Thai Lullaby* by Minfong Ho. New York: Orchard, 1996.**

A mother scolds all the animals to be quiet so that her baby can sleep. After reading the story, ask the children if their parents sing to them before they go to sleep. What kinds of animals would their parents scold to be quiet?

**19**  ***A South African Night* by Rachel Isadora. New York: Greenwillow, 1998.**

Gentle illustrations and simple text celebrate the human and animal life of South Africa.

**20**  ***Hula Lullaby* by Erin Eitter Kono. New York: Little, Brown, 2005.**

A mother sings a gentle bedtime song of Hawaii in this lilting, rhyming book. Follow up by playing Hawaiian music and inviting the children to sway and hula.

**21**  ***Counting Ovejas* by Sarah Weeks. New York: Atheneum, 2006.**

When a young boy can't sleep, an increasing number of sheep appear in his room. As he works to remove the colorful sheep, he eventually becomes tired enough to sleep. He sends the sheep away using Spanish to announce their numbers and colors. After reading the story, use a simple flannelboard of sheep in various colors to review the Spanish vocabulary and retell the story.

# Flannelboards

## 22 *Siesta* by Ginger Foglesong Guy. New York: HarperCollins, 2005.

A little boy looks for everything he needs to take a siesta. Simple text in English and Spanish introduces Spanish vocabulary for naptime items.

## 23 What Type of Bed Do You Use?

What type of bed do you use
To close your eyes and take a snooze?
If I'm in Japan and want to sleep,
A futon is what I need to keep.
In the jungle, I sleep high in the trees,
In a hammock where the animals can't see.
In Africa I sleep on a mat.
When I'm tired I unroll it from where it sat.
Here in America when I lay my head,
I need pillows placed upon my bed.

# Fingerplays and Songs

### 24 *Siesta (see-ESS-tah)

We take a break from our morning fun,
To eat our lunch and get out of the sun.
With our stomachs full of our mom's best,
We find that it's time to take a rest.
A nap is what we need today,
A *siesta* before we go back out to play.

### 25 *Good Night Song (to the tune of "Good Night, Ladies")

Teach the signs, and then invite the children to join you in singing and signing the song.

Good night, mommies, good night, mommies,
Good night, mommies, it's time to say good night.
Good night, daddies . . .
Good night, children . . .

### 26 *Too-Ra-Loo-Ra-Loo-Ral: A Traditional Irish Lullaby

Teach the children this simple traditional tune. (If you are unfamiliar with the tune, you can hear it at www .kididdles.com/lyrics/i011.html). Then pass out ribbons or scarves and invite the children to wave them slow, fast, and medium as you sing the song at various speeds. Ask the children which way would be best to sing the song to help a baby feel sleepy. This activity enhances phonemic awareness, gross motor development, and understanding of contrast.

Too-ra-loo-ra-loo-ral, too-ra-loo-ra-li,
Too-ra-loo-ra-loo-ral, hush now don't you cry!
Too-ra-loo-ra-loo-ral, too-ra-loo-ra-li,
Too-ra-loo-ra-loo-ral, that's an Irish lullaby.

# Craft

### 27 Dreamcatcher

The Ojibwa (Chippewa) used dreamcatchers as a charm to protect sleeping children from bad dreams. Traditional dreamcatchers were made by stringing sinew in a web around a circular or tear-shaped frame. This version is easy enough for children to make in storytime.

*Materials:* paper plates, yarn, hole punch, tape, crayons or markers, feathers, beads, stickers or other decorating materials

*Preparation:*

1. Cut out the center of each paper plate so that you are left with a ring.
2. Punch holes every inch or two around the inside of the plate. The fewer holes you punch the easier the craft will be, so punch fewer holes for younger children and more holes for older children.
3. Punch one hole in the top of each plate (for the hanger) and one hole in the bottom of each plate (for the dangling feathers).
4. Cut the following lengths of yarn for each child, in whatever colors you choose:
    one 32-inch piece of yarn for the center web of the dreamcatcher (this piece may need to be longer if you have punched more holes in the plate)
    two 16-inch pieces of yarn, one for the hanger and one for the piece that dangles at the bottom
5. Wrap a piece of tape around one end of the longest piece of yarn, to make it easier for the children to thread it through the holes.

*Directions:*

1. Decorate the paper plate ring using crayons, markers, stickers, etc.
2. Take the long piece of yarn and pull it through one of the holes. Tape the end to the back of the plate so it doesn't pull all the way through.
3. Thread the yarn back and forth across the plate and through the holes to create a web. If desired, thread beads along the yarn as you do this so that they decorate the web.
4. When you reach the end of the yarn, thread it so that the loose piece is in the back and then tape it securely to the back of the plate.
5. Thread one of the shorter pieces of yarn through the top hole in the plate and knot it to make a hanger.
6. Thread the other piece of yarn through the bottom hole in the plate and let the ends hang down.
7. Glue, tape, or tie feathers and beads onto the dangling pieces.

# 4

# Big and Little

∙∙∙∙∙∙∙∙∙∙∙∙∙∙∙∙∙∙∙∙∙∙∙∙∙∙∙∙∙∙∙∙∙∙∙∙∙∙∙∙∙∙∙

## Books

**28** *Fin M'Coul: The Giant of Knockmany Hill* **by Tomie dePaola. New York: Holiday House, 1981.**

In this funny Irish tall tale, Fin M'Coul and his wife outsmart the giant Cucullin.

**29** *The Teeny-Tiny Woman* **by Paul Galdone. New York: Clarion, 1984.**

This rhythmic rendition of a traditional, spooky-but-not-too-spooky English ghost story is just right for preschoolers.

**30** *\*The Lion and the Mouse* **by Jerry Pinkney. New York: Little, Brown, 2009.**

Through illustrations, this 2010 Caldecott Medal winner retells Aesop's fable of a little mouse who saves a big lion.

**31** *Abiyoyo* **by Pete Seeger. New York: Macmillan, 1986.**

Based on an old South African folktale, this book tells the story of a father and son who face down Abiyoyo, the great, scary, smelly giant who terrorizes the small town. With its musical refrain that tames the giant, this story invites audience participation.

## Flannelboard

**32** *Leola and the Honeybears* **by Melodye Benson Rosales. New York: Cartwheel, 1999.**

In this African American retelling of "Goldilocks and the Three Bears," Leola wanders into the Honeybears' Inn after being frightened by Ol' Mister Weasel.

## Fingerplays and Songs

**33** **Big and Little: A Spanish Game**

Introduce the following Spanish vocabulary, then show a variety of objects and ask the children to identify their sizes by using their new Spanish words.

> big: *grande* (GRAHN-deh)
> little: *pequeño* (peh-KEH-nyo)

### 34 *Little Mouse: A Nursery Rhyme from China

Reprinted with permission from *Chinese and English Nursery Rhymes* by Faye-Lynn Wu (North Clarendon, VT: Tuttle, 2010).

Recite the following rhyme and ask the children if it reminds them of a nursery rhyme they know. Discuss how the rhyme is similar to and different from "Hickory Dickory Dock."

The little mouse climbed up the lamp
To find some oil to nibble.
Can't get down,
Meow, meow, meow.
Here came the cat,
*Ji-li-gu-lu*, down fell the mouse.

### 35 *Cookie Song (to the tune of "Pop! Goes the Weasel")

Teach the following signs, and then use them as you sing the song.

My mom and I decide to BAKE.
We make ourselves a COOKIE.
It goes in the oven and then we WAIT.
Crunch (EAT) goes the COOKIE!
But . . . then we decide to make a really big COOKIE!

Repeat song in a loud voice, with very large signs.

Then we decide to make a teeny tiny COOKIE!

Repeat song in a tiny voice, with very small signs.

# Craft

### 36 *Leola and the Honeybears* Stick Puppets

Based on the story *Leola and the Honeybears* by Melodye Benson Rosales (New York: Cartwheel, 1999).

*Materials:* stick puppet template (from website), craft sticks, glue, crayons, scissors

*Directions:*

1. Color the background sheet and characters.
2. Cut out the characters.
3. Glue the characters to craft sticks.
4. Retell the story with the stick puppets.

# 5 Birds

· · · · · · · · · · · · · · · · · · · · · · · · · · · · · · · · · · · ·

## Books

**37 *Honey . . . Honey . . . Lion!* by Jan Brett. New York: Putnam, 2005.**

The true story and legend of the honeyguide bird and badger are told in this tale from Botswana. After reading, ask the children to help retell the story, asking prompting questions such as:

> What does the honeyguide do for the badger?
> What did the badger do to make the honeyguide mad?
> How did the honeyguide teach the badger a lesson?

**38 *\*The Perfect Nest* by Catherine Friend. Cambridge, MA: Candlewick, 2007.**

Jack the cat is building a perfect nest to attract the perfect bird, who will then lay the perfect egg for his breakfast. But Jack is surprised to find he attracts more than one perfect bird—he attracts three perfect birds, each claiming the nest for itself. The text incorporates Spanish and French vocabulary. As you read, ask the children to guess where different birds came from using the text clues.

**39 *Island Baby* by Holly Keller. New York: Greenwillow, 1992.**

Young Simon helps out Pops, who runs a bird hospital on his Caribbean island. But when Simon finds an injured baby flamingo, he becomes attached.

**40 *Rechenka's Eggs* by Patricia Polacco. New York: Philomel, 1988.**

In this lovely story set in old Moscow, Babushka takes in an injured goose, never dreaming that it will produce miraculously designed eggs for her to take to the festival.

# Flannelboards

### 41 *Kookaburra: A Traditional Australian Song

You can hear a recording of this song on *Bridges Across the World: A Multicultural Songfest* by Sarah Barchas (Sonoita, AZ: High Haven Music, 1999).

Kookaburra sits in the old gum tree,
Merry, merry king of the bush is he.
Laugh, Kookaburra,
Laugh, Kookaburra,
Glad your life must be!

Kookaburra sits in the old gum tree,
Eating all the gumdrops he can see.
Stop, Kookaburra,
Stop, Kookaburra,
Leave some there for me!

### 42 How the Baby Birds Learned to Fly: A Folktale from Sri Lanka

Sri Lanka is a tropical island that lies just south of India. A beautiful bird called the fairy bluebird lives there. Well, once upon a time a mama fairy bluebird built a little nest inside a little hole in a tree. Her nest looked like a little cup, and it was made from moss and twigs. She laid one, two eggs in it, and she waited. And waited. And waited.

Finally, one day, she felt something tap tap tapping.

A little bird poked its head out!

Tap, tap, tap!

Another little bird poked its head out.

Mama Bird snuggled close to her babies to keep them warm. Then she fed them some yummy bugs, and even yummier fruit! Fairy bluebirds love fruit!

Those two little birds ate all those bugs and the fruit right up and they grew . . . and grew . . . and grew! Finally they were so big that they were ready to learn how to fly.

But . . . uh-oh! They were so big that they couldn't fit through the hole in the tree!

Mama Bird looked down and saw a carpenter walking by. She called to him, "Carpenter, please! Use your hammer to make the hole bigger so my babies can come out and learn how to fly!"

The carpenter grumbled, "No. Why should I?"

So Mama Bird called to the snake. "Please bite the big toe of the carpenter so he will use his hammer to make the hole bigger so my babies can come out and learn how to fly!"

The snake hissed, "No! Why should I?"

So Mama Bird called to the elephant. "Please step on the tail of the snake so he will bite the big toe of the carpenter so he will use his hammer to make the hole bigger so my babies can come out and learn how to fly!"

The elephant trumpeted, "No! Why should I?"

So Mama Bird called to the mouse. "Please tickle the elephant so he will step on the tail of the snake so the snake will bite the big toe of the carpenter so he will use his hammer to make the hole bigger so my babies can come out and learn how to fly!"

The mouse squeaked, "No! Why should I?"

So Mama Bird called to the cat. "Please chase the mouse up the elephant's trunk so the mouse will tickle the elephant so the elephant will step on the tail of the snake so the snake will bite the big toe of the carpenter so he will use his hammer to make the hole bigger so my babies can come out and learn how to fly!"

The cat purred, "Sure! I love to chase mice!"

So the cat chased the mouse up elephant's trunk, tickling the elephant. The elephant laughed so hard that he stepped on the snake's tail. The snake was so angry that he bit the carpenter's toe. The carpenter jumped up and down and said, "Fine, I will make the hole bigger!" And he did! Then the two baby birds came out of their nest and learned how to fly.

# Fingerplays and Songs

### 43 *Little Bird: A Rhyme from India

Bird comes (*hold palm out flat, show bird flying to palm with index finger and thumb of other hand*)
Eats some seed (*make bird eat seeds from palm*)
Drinks a little water (*lift index finger and thumb as if bird is drinking*)
And flies away! (*make bird fly away*)

### 44 So Many Eggs

Place pictures of a robin, a penguin, a parrot, an emu, and an ostrich inside plastic eggs, then place the eggs in a nest made from crumpled brown paper. Each time you say the rhyme, open one egg and insert the bird's name into the rhyme. Discuss where in the world each animal can be found. When you are finished opening all the eggs, tell the children that there are many more animals that hatch from eggs, and ask if they can name any.

I found a nest while walking one day.
"Look at all the eggs!" I had to say.
I waited and waited and what did I see?
Craaaack! Who hatched? A baby _____ was looking at me!

### 45 *Los Pollitos Dicen / The Baby Chicks Are Singing

This traditional Spanish tune can be found on *De Colores and Other Latin American Folk Songs* by Jose-Luis Orozco (Berkeley, CA: Arcoiris Records, 2009).
    If you are overwhelmed by the idea of teaching the whole song in Spanish, then teach the children only the first line in Spanish and sing the rest of the song in English.

*Los pollitos dicen pío, pío, pío* (LOS pol-YEE-toes DEE-sen PEE-o PEE-o PEE-o)
*Cuando tienen hambre, Cuando tienen frío* (COOAHN-doe TEE-eh-nen AHM-bray, COOAHN-doe
    TEE-eh-nen FREE-o)
*La gallina busca el maíz y el trigo.* (la gahl-YEE-nah BOOSE-cah el mah-EESS ee el TREE-go)
*Les da la comida y les presta abrigo.* (les dah la co-MEE-dah ee les PRES-tah ah-BREE-go)
*Bajo sus dos alas, acurrucaditos,* (BAH-ho soos dos AHL-as AH-cu-roo-cah-DEE-toes)
*Hasta el otro día duermen los pollitos!* (AHS-tah el O-tro DEE-ah DUER-men los pol-YEE-toes)

The baby chicks are singing peep, peep, peep,
The baby chicks are hungry and are too cold to sleep.
The mother hen, she looks and looks for corn and wheat.
She kisses her hungry babies, and gives them food to eat.
Safe under Mama's wings, cuddling and keeping warm,
The baby chicks can sleep safe and sound 'til morn!

# Craft

### 46  What Bird Is That?

*Materials:* eggshell pieces from template (from website), pictures of birds (from website), crayons, glue, paper fasteners

*Directions:*

1. Choose a bird and color the picture.
2. Glue the bird to the bottom half of the egg so that it pokes up in the middle.
3. Attach the top of the egg to the bottom using a paper fastener.
4. Share the rhyme on the egg with someone and crack open the egg to see the bird!

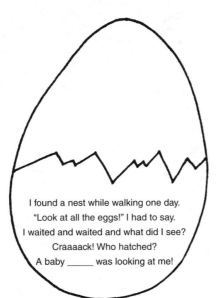

I found a nest while walking one day.
"Look at all the eggs!" I had to say.
I waited and waited and what did I see?
Craaaack! Who hatched?
A baby _____ was looking at me!

# 6
# Books and Libraries

. . . . . . . . . . . . . . . . . . . . . . . . . . . . . . . . . . . . . . . . . .

## Books

**47**  *That Book Woman* **by Heather Henson. New York: Atheneum, 2008.**

Cal is not the reading type. He does not have much use for the books his sister devours or for the Book Woman who rides her horse up the mountain to his Appalachia home every two weeks to bring new books that come "free as air." Gradually, though, he realizes how brave the Book Woman and her horse are and wants to find out what could be worth that arduous trip. This lovely book is a tribute to the Pack Horse Librarians of 1930s Kentucky.

**48**  *\*Book Fiesta* **by Pat Mora. New York: HarperCollins, 2009.**

Through rhyming text in English and Spanish, children celebrate the Mexican celebration of the Day of the Child (April 30) by reading their favorite books.

**49**  *\*Biblioburro: A True Story from Colombia* **by Jeanette Winter. New York: Beach Lane Books, 2010.**

Luis and his donkeys travel from village to village in Colombia sharing books.

**50**  *The Librarian of Basra: A True Story from Iraq* **by Jeanette Winter. New York: Harcourt, 2005.**

When the invasion of Iraq reached Basra, the library burned to the ground. But librarian Alia Muhammad Baker managed to smuggle 70 percent of the library's collection into the homes of her family and friends to wait for the day when the library would be rebuilt.

## Flannelboard

### 51 *My Library

My library is different from yours:
In Australia a truck pulls up and opens its doors.
My library can be found on the sea:
In Finland I visit the boat docked just for me.
My library travels across a desert canyon:
In Mongolia I look in a passing horse-drawn wagon.
My library reaches me on a mountain settlement:
In Thailand books arrive on the back of an elephant.
My library is on the road five days a week:
In Kenya the camel travels regardless of heat.

## Fingerplays and Songs

### 52 Everybody's Library: A Guessing Game

Miss Lisa wants to help everyone find a book.
   Juan approaches the desk and asks, "*Libro?*" (LEE-bro)
   Do you know what Juan wants? (book) Do you know what language he speaks? (Spanish)
   Miss Lisa gets Juan his book, and he says, "*Gracias.*" (GRAH-see-ahs) (thank you)
   Here comes Suzette. "*Livre?*" (LEE-vruh)
   Do you know what Suzette wants? (book) Do you know what language she speaks? (French)
   Miss Lisa gets Suzette her book, and she says, "*Merci!*" (mare-SEE) (thank you)
   Ping approaches the desk and asks, "*Shū?*" (shoo)
   Do you know what Ping wants? (book) Do you know what language he speaks? (Chinese)
   Miss Lisa gets Ping his book, and he says, "*Xie xie.*" (sheh sheh) (thank you)
   Gretchen stands at the desk and says, "*Buch?*" (bookh)
   Do you know what Gretchen wants? (book) Do you know what language she speaks? (German)
   Miss Lisa gets Gretchen her book, and she says, "*Danke.*" (DONK-eh) (thank you)

Tammy stands at the desk and signs:

Do you know what Tammy wants? (book) Do you know what language she uses? (American Sign Language)

Miss Lisa gets Tammy her book, and she signs:

### 53 *Libro* Dance

Introduce *libro* (LEE-bro), the Spanish word for "book." Give each child a book and follow the actions in the rhyme.

If your *libro* is red, put it on your head.
If your *libro* is blue, put it on your shoe.
If your *libro* is yellow, put it on a fellow.
If your *libro* is brown, wave it up and down.
If your *libro* is black, put it on your back.
If your *libro* is green, wipe it clean.
If your *libro* is pink, hold it up and wink.
If your *libro* is a book, raise it up and look.

### 54 "These Are My Glasses" from *Whaddaya Think of That?* by Laurie Berkner. New York: Two Tomatoes, 2000.

Lyrics reprinted with permission.

This simple song is a great way to introduce basic American Sign Language. The four basic signs in this song demonstrate how movement can change the meaning of a sign. Introduce the following signs, and then show the children the song.

1. EYEGLASSES: The noun EYEGLASSES has a double movement. To make this sign into the verb TAKE-OFF-EYEGLASSES, start the sign at your face and show the glasses being taken off in a single movement. For the verb PUT-ON-EYEGLASSES, start the sign away from your face and show the glasses being put on, again in a single movement.

2. BOOK: The noun BOOK has a double movement (as a book opening and closing). To make this sign into the verb OPEN-BOOK, start with your palms together and then let them fall open with a single movement. For the verb CLOSE-BOOK, start with your palms lying open, then close them with a single movement.

3. READ: Hold up one hand flat to represent the page. The V-shape of the other hand points to the page and moves up and down, like eyes moving over the page.

4. LOOK: This sign is similar to READ, but the V-shape moves directly toward and away from the page instead of moving up and down. Notice how the difference in movement changes the meaning. In American Sign Language, as in sign languages all over the world, the meaning of a sign depends on handshape, movement, location, and facial expression, instead of on sounds.

These are my glasses (EYEGLASSES),
This is my book (BOOK).
I put on my glasses (PUT-ON-EYEGLASSES)
And open up the book (OPEN-BOOK).
Then I read, read, read (READ READ READ)
And I look, look, look (LOOK LOOK LOOK).
I take off my glasses (TAKE-OFF-EYEGLASSES)
And close up the book (CLOSE-BOOK).

# Craft

### 55 Papyrus

In ancient Egypt, paper was made from a reed called *papyrus*. This craft duplicates the process of making papyrus paper, using brown paper strips in place of the flattened reeds.

*Materials:* brown craft paper or brown paper bags ripped into strips, a bowl containing equal parts white glue and water, damp rags, paper towels

*Directions:*

1. Lay a paper towel out to work on.
2. Dip a strip of brown paper into the glue and water mixture.

3. Lay the strip vertically on the paper towel.
4. Continue to dip strips into the mixture and lay them vertically on the paper towel, with their edges overlapping.
5. Take a damp rag and run it vertically over the strips to remove excess glue and water.
6. Dip more strips into the mixture and lay them horizontally over the vertical strips so that their edges overlap.
7. Run the damp rag over the horizontal strips to remove excess moisture.
8. Let the paper dry, then peel off the paper towel and use your paper to write or create a scroll. (For easy transport home from storytime, slide the paper towel and paper onto a paper plate.)

# 7
# Brothers and Sisters

· · · · · · · · · · · · · · · · · · · · · · · · · · · · · · · ·

## Books

**56** *Ian's Walk: A Story about Autism* **by Laurie Lears. Morton Grove, IL: Whitman, 1998.**

A little girl is initially embarrassed by her little brother, who is autistic, but when he goes missing and she has to think like him in order to find him, she begins to understand him better.

**57** *Adele and Simon* **by Barbara McClintock. New York: Worzalla, 2006.**

As Adele walks her brother, Simon, home from school, they make various stops throughout Paris. At each stop, Simon loses something. Luckily, after the pair reaches home, people from each stop line up at the door to return each of Simon's items. Spend some time discussing the illustrations with the children, using the notes in the back of the book.

**58** *\*Three Pandas* **by Jan Wahl. Honesdale, PA: Boyds Mills Press, 2000.**

Three sibling pandas living in the bamboo forest of China decide to explore the city. When they find that the city isn't all they imagined, they realize there is no place like home!

**59** *Brothers* **by Yin. New York: Philomel, 2006.**

In the mid-1800s, a Chinese boy immigrates to San Francisco to work in his brother's store in China-town. There he meets and becomes friends with an Irish immigrant boy who teaches him English. Soon the two communities are joined, and the store is serving customers of many backgrounds.

# Flannelboard

## 60  The Seven Chinese Brothers: A Tale from China

Adapted from the book by Margaret Mahy (New York: Scholastic, 1990).

Once, in China, there were seven brothers. Each brother had an amazing talent. The first brother had incredible hearing. The second brother could see things a hundred miles away. The third brother was very strong and could lift mountains. The fourth had bones that couldn't break. The fifth brother had legs as long as tree trunks. The sixth brother never became too hot. And when the seventh brother wept, each of his tears would fill a river.

Fortunately, Seventh Brother rarely had anything to cry about, because he and his brothers had a happy life together. But one day as they were on the hillside working, First Brother heard something far away. He said, "I hear moaning and groaning a hundred miles away, by the Great Wall of China. Second Brother, look and tell me what all the trouble is."

Second Brother looked. "Oh, no!" he cried. "I see a huge hole in the Great Wall of China! A hundred poor men are working to fix it. They look so tired and weak."

"Oh! That is so sad!" said Seventh Brother.

"Don't cry!" said Third Brother quickly. "I'll go and help them." He walked the hundred miles quickly, lifting up mountains and setting them back down after he passed.

When he got to the Great Wall, he used his great strength to lift stones and set them into the hole. The wall was repaired by sunset.

Third Brother was tired, so he lay down and took a nap.

But when the emperor heard that one man had repaired the hole, and so quickly, he was worried.

"A man as powerful as that may try to become emperor in my place," thought the emperor. "I will send two armies to catch him."

When Third Brother woke up from his nap, he was surrounded by two armies! The general told him that the emperor had ordered him to be executed in the morning. Third Brother started to cry. A hundred miles away, First Brother heard this. Second Brother looked far into the distance.

"Oh, no! Third Brother is surrounded by two armies! They are going to execute him in the morning. That is why he is crying."

"I know!" cried Fourth Brother. "I will change places with him. The emperor can try cutting off my head, but my bones will not break!"

Off he went. He sneaked in between the two armies and took Third Brother's place. Third Brother went home.

The next day the officers tried again and again to behead Fourth Brother, but no sword would cut through his bones of iron. The soldiers told the emperor that they simply could not behead their prisoner.

The emperor was frightened. "Drown him in the sea tomorrow!" he cried.

When Fourth Brother heard that, he wept with fear. A hundred miles away, First Brother heard, and Second Brother looked into the distance. "Oh, no! Tomorrow morning they are going to drown Fourth Brother!"

"I know!" Fifth Brother said. "I will change places with him. They can try to drown me, but it will not work, because my legs are so long."

Off he went to take Fourth Brother's place, and Fourth Brother went home.

The next day the soldiers tried to drown Fifth Brother, but his legs grew so long that the water only came to his knees.

The emperor was even more frightened. "Throw him into the fire tomorrow morning!" he commanded.

Fifth Brother burst into tears. A hundred miles away, First Brother heard, and Second Brother looked into the distance. "Oh, no! Tomorrow morning they are going to burn Fifth Brother."

"I know!" said Sixth Brother. "I will take his place. They can burn me all day long, but I can never get too hot."

Off he went. He took Fifth Brother's place, and Fifth Brother went home.

The next day the two armies built a huge fire. They made Sixth Brother stand in it, but he felt pleasantly cool. The emperor was furious. "In the morning we will shoot this man full of arrows!" he cried.

Sixth Brother burst into tears. A hundred miles away, First Brother heard, and Second Brother looked into the distance. "Oh, no! Tomorrow morning they are going to shoot Sixth Brother full of arrows."

The brothers looked at each other. "There is nothing we can do," said First Brother. "But we can-not leave Sixth Brother to die alone. We will all go to the emperor. He can shoot arrows through all of us. At least we will be together."

The brothers went to the palace, but poor Seventh Brother was so upset that he couldn't help cry-ing a little. A great ocean of warm salt water swept down the road ahead of the brothers. It swept on for a hundred miles. Seventh Brother's first tear swept away one army north. His second tear swept the other army south. And the emperor was tossed so high and so far that he was never seen again.

Sixth Brother was free! He hurried back up the road and met his brothers coming down the road.

# Fingerplays and Songs

### 61  Brothers and Sisters

Before beginning this chant, introduce the following Spanish vocabulary:

brothers: *hermanos* (air-MAH-nos)
sisters: *hermanas* (air-MAH-nahs)

Brothers and sisters, sisters and brothers,
We all try to get along.
Sisters and brothers, brothers and sisters,
Keep it up and clap along.
*Hermanos y hermanas, hermanas y hermanos,*
We all try to get along.
*Hermanas y hermanos, hermanos y hermanas,*
Keep it up and clap along.

Repeat entire rhyme, increasing speed.

### 62  Sibling Song: A Song in ASL and English (to the tune of "The Bear Went Over the Mountain")

I love my brother.
I love my brother.
I love my brother.
We love to play.

I love my sister.
I love my sister.
I love my sister.
We love to play.

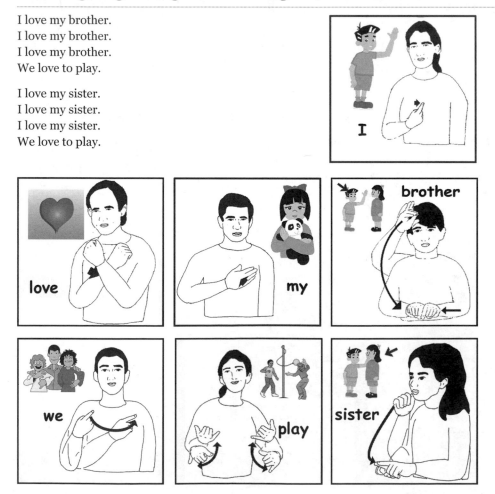

**63  Jack and Jill** (traditional)

Jack and Jill went up the hill
To fetch a pail of water.
Jack fell down and cracked his crown,
And Jill came tumbling after.

Then up Jack got, and home did trot,
As fast as he could caper.
They put him to bed and plaster'd his head
With vinegar and brown paper.

# Craft

**64  Rakhi Celebration Bracelets**

In northern India, Rakhi (also known as Raksha Bandhan) is a celebration of the special relationship between brothers and sisters. The festival is celebrated on the full moon day of the fifth month of the Hindu lunisolar calendar. On Rakhi, sisters tie a bracelet of silver or gold thread around the wrists of their brothers, symbolizing the never-dying relationship between brothers and sisters.

*Materials:* yarn or embroidery floss, scissors, beads (optional)

*Directions:*

1. Precut lengths of yarn or floss for each child.
2. Braid or twist together strands of yarn or floss. If desired, string beads along the thread.
3. Tie the ends together to make a bracelet. Cut off the excess yarn or floss.

# 8

# Bugs and Insects

· · · · · · · · · · · · · · · · · · · · · · · · · · · · · · · · · · · · · ·

## Books

**65** *Why Mosquitoes Buzz in People's Ears: A West African Tale* **by Verna Aardema. New York: Dial, 1975.**

When Mosquito annoys Iguana with her chatter, the consequences spread out across the forest in this amusing pourquoi tale from Africa.

**66** *Martina the Beautiful Cockroach: A Cuban Folktale* **by Carmen Agra Deedy. Atlanta: Peachtree, 2007.**

In this Pura Belpré Honor Book, Martina the cockroach is ready to give her leg in marriage. On the advice of her grandmother, she splashes coffee on each of her suitors to see if they react angrily. She finds her perfect match, though not the way she expects.

**67** *Anansi and the Magic Stick* **by Eric A. Kimmel. New York: Holiday House, 2001.**

In this African folktale, Anansi the spider steals Hyena's magic stick. But when Anansi falls asleep while the magic stick is watering his garden, he causes a flood that the animals learn to love. After reading, invite the children to imagine that they have magic sticks and to name what jobs their sticks would do.

**68** *\*Buzz Buzz Buzz* **by Verónica Uribe. Toronto, ON: Groundwood Books, 2001.**

When two children in a South American jungle are trying to sleep, a mosquito's buzzing keeps them awake. Finally, they run through the jungle trying to escape the mosquito and begging for help from the different animals they encounter.

# Flannelboard

### 69  How Beetle Got Her Beautiful Coat: A Folktale from Brazil

In Brazil, beetles have beautiful hard shells of green and gold. But it wasn't always so. Years ago, Beetle was plain brown.

One day, a long time ago, Beetle was crawling along when up ran a big gray rat. Rat looked down at Beetle and said, "You crawl so slowly! I bet you wish you could run as fast as I can!"

Rat ran off and then came back, to show her how fast he was.

"Yes, friend Rat," said Beetle politely. "You are very fast."

Nearby, a big green and gold parrot sat in a tree. Parrot did not like the boastful way that Rat spoke, so he said, "Beetle, why don't you and Rat have a race? I will offer a beautiful new coat to the winner."

Rat laughed. "I would like that new coat. Surely I will win."

Beetle said, "Very well, Rat, I will race you. But I think I would like a new coat, too."

Rat just laughed again.

Parrot told them that they would race to the big palm tree at the top of the cliff. Beetle and Rat lined up, then Parrot said, "Ready . . . set . . . go!"

Rat and Beetle took off. Rat ran as fast as he could, and soon he looked around and couldn't see Beetle anymore. "I am winning!" he cried. He decided to slow down. After all, he was so far ahead he could afford to rest.

Once he had gotten his breath, Rat ran to the finish line.

When he got to the big palm tree at the top of the cliff he couldn't believe his eyes! There was Beetle, right next to Parrot!

"How did you manage to get here first?" Rat said. "I know you can't run faster than I can."

The little brown beetle drew out the tiny wings from her sides. "No one said anything about running," she said. "I flew."

"I didn't know you could fly," said Rat. He felt silly.

"Beetle has won the race!" said Parrot. "Rat, I hope you have learned your lesson about judging others by their looks alone."

Parrot presented Beetle with a beautiful coat of green and gold, which she still wears today. But even now, in Brazil where all the animals and flowers are so brightly colored, Rat is still a dull gray.

## Fingerplays and Songs

### 70 *La Araña Pequeñita* / **The Itsy-Bitsy Spider**

Introduce the phrase *la araña pequeñita* (la ah-RAHN-yah peh-keh-NYEE-tah), and then sing the following song. Ask the children to guess what this Spanish phrase means. Then invite the children to sing with you.

*La araña pequeñita*
Climbed up the waterspout.
Down came the rain
And washed *la araña* out.
Out came the sun
And dried up all the rain.
*La araña pequeñita*
Climbed up the spout again.

### 71 **The Little Spider: A Nursery Rhyme from the Philippines**

The little spider, the little spider (*wiggle index finger*)
Climbed up the branch. (*move index finger up opposite arm*)
The rain came down, (*wiggle fingers down*)
Pushed it away. (*show spider falling*)
The sun came up. (*hold arms in circle over head*)
It dried the branch.
The little spider is always happy. (*make index finger hop up arm again*)

### 72 **Caterpillar, Caterpillar: An Action Rhyme in ASL and English**

CATERPILLAR, caterpillar, turn around.
Caterpillar, caterpillar, touch the ground.
Caterpillar, caterpillar, reach up high.
Soon you'll be a BUTTERFLY!

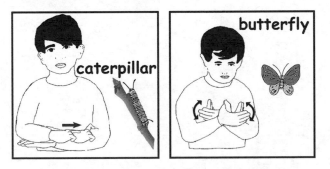

### 73 **"La Cucaracha" from *I Have a Dream: World Music for Children* by Daria Marmaluk-Hajioannou. Riegelsville, PA: Dariamusic, 2009.**

In alternating English and Spanish verses, this song tells of the little cockroach. Pass out maracas and encourage children to dance to the beat!

# Craft

### 74 **Monarch Butterfly**

Monarch butterflies migrate from as far as Canada to Mexico in early November. They stay until March, when they begin their journey north again.

*Materials:* coffee filter, orange, brown, black, red, and yellow washable markers, spring clothespin, spray bottle of water

*Directions:*

1. Decorate the coffee filter using markers.
2. Lightly spray each filter with water to allow the marker colors to spread through the filter.
3. Allow the coffee filter to dry.
4. Gather the filter in the center and clip with a spring clothespin.
5. Draw eyes on the clothespin.

# 9
# Cats and Dogs

## Books

**75 *Temple Cat* by Andrew Clements. New York: Clarion, 1996.**

A temple cat in ancient Egypt longs for genuine affection instead of worship, so he runs away into the city. Before reading the story, explain that cats were worshipped as gods in ancient Egypt. After reading the story, ask the children how they would feel if they lived in the temple like the cat. Would they want to escape and live an ordinary life? Why or why not? Share more facts about cats in ancient Egypt (one good source is www.ancientegyptonline.co.uk/cat.html). Ask how many of the children have cats at home. Why do they think that the Egyptians worshipped cats instead of another animal?

**76 *Anna and Natalie* by Barbara H. Cole. New York: Star Bright, 2007.**

Anna is a little girl who is blind, and Natalie is her seeing-eye dog—but that's not the focus of this moving story. Four students from Anna's class will be chosen to lay a wreath on the Tomb of the Unknown Soldier at Arlington National Cemetery, and all the children have to write letters to convince the teacher that they should be chosen. Anna writes her letter on Natalie's behalf, asking to be part of the team in order to represent the canine heroes of World War II, who carried medicine and food to soldiers. Anna's blindness and reliance on a seeing-eye dog are background to the story, but the book is a satisfying portrayal of a character any child can relate to.

**77 *Owney, the Mail-Pouch Pooch* by Mona Kerby. New York: Farrar, Straus and Giroux, 2008.**

In 1888, Owney, a stray dog, made his home in the Albany, New York, post office. Owney had no desire to become a pet. Instead he preferred to ride the mail trains, protecting the mail that was being delivered across the United States. In time, he even rode boats carrying mail to foreign countries. Use a map of the United States and the world to track Owney's travels. Ask the children what they think of Owney's adventures.

78  *Pino and the Signora's Pasta* by Janet Pedersen. Cambridge, MA: Candlewick, 2005.

The Signora brings pasta each night for Pino and his cat friends, but on this night, Pino wants to sample something new. He prowls the streets of Rome, but none of the diners wants to share with him. At last he returns to the Signora who loves him. Point out the Italian words in the text and ask if the children can guess what they mean from the context.

# Flannelboards

79  **Fat Cat: A Danish Folktale**

Once upon a time there were a cat and a mouse. They were friends. The one problem with this relationship was that the cat was always hungry. And you know what cats like to eat. Fortunately, the mouse loved to cook. One day the mouse made a giant pie for the cat. The cat ate it in one gulp!

"I am still hungry!" said the cat. So he went outside. There he saw an old woman washing clothes.

"My," said the old woman. "You are a fat cat!"

The cat said, "I am the Fat Cat. I ate the pie, and now I will eat you, just like that!"

And he ate up the old woman, and her laundry, too! (*replace small cat with medium cat*)

But the cat was still hungry!

Up marched three soldiers. "My," said the soldiers. "You are a fat cat!"

The cat said, "I am the Fat Cat. I ate the pie, and the old woman, and now I will eat you, just like that!"

And he ate up the soldiers, and their swords, too! (*replace medium cat with larger cat*)

The cat walked along until he ran into the king riding his elephant.

"My," said the king. "You are a fat cat!"

The cat said, "I am the Fat Cat. I ate the pie, and the old woman, and the three soldiers, and now I will eat you, just like that!"

And he ate up the king, and his elephant, too! (*replace larger cat with extra-large cat*)

The cat was still feeling hungry, and he turned toward home.

When he got there, the mouse looked up from her sewing and said, "My, you are a fat cat!"

The cat said, "I am the Fat Cat. I ate the pie, and I ate the old woman, and I ate the soldiers, and I ate the king, and his elephant, too, and now I will eat you, just like that!"

And he ate up the mouse, and her scissors, needle, and thread, too.

The mouse got mad. "I know you're hungry, but really, enough is enough!" she said.

She took her scissors, and she cut a little hole in the cat's belly.

Out popped the mouse!

Out popped the king and his elephant!

Out popped the three soldiers and their swords!

Out popped the old woman and her laundry!

They all went about their business.

The mouse spent the rest of the day sewing up the cat's tummy. But first, the cat had to promise that he would eat only cat food from then on!

## 80  *Why Cat and Rat Are Enemies: A Story from the Democratic Republic of the Congo

Adapted from "Cat and Rat" in *Meow: Cat Stories from Around the World* by Jane Yolen (New York: HarperCollins, 2005).

Long, long ago, Cat and Rat lived together on an island. They played and sang together in the sun. Cat had plenty of birds in the trees to eat. Rat loved to eat nuts and a plant called *manioc* that grew on the island, so he was never hungry either.

But for all that, Cat and Rat were not satisfied. They became bored with the little island and decided to go exploring. Rat had the idea to carve a boat out of manioc root, because the manioc was so sturdy and tough. So they did. Then they carved paddles for themselves as well.

When all was ready, they climbed into the boat. They rowed out into the sea, away from their island.

They rowed all afternoon while the sun rose high overhead.

They heard a noise. It sounded like this: grrrrrr.

"What was that?" said Cat.

"Maybe it's a monster!" said Rat. "Let's keep rowing to get away from it."

They rowed faster, but the noise came again, louder this time. GRRRRRRR.

"Oh!" said Rat. "The monster is closer, and it makes my stomach hurt."

"My stomach hurts, too!" said Cat. "Oh, what could it be?"

And then they realized that they hadn't brought any food along with them. Neither of them had eaten since breakfast, and their bellies were rumbling so loudly it sounded like a monster chasing them!

Cat and Rat cried out loud, because they were so hungry. But of course crying does not put food in your belly. They were stuck in the middle of the sea, far away from land. So they curled up and went to sleep, trying to forget about their hollow tummies.

Rat woke up from a dream about eating manioc, and he sat straight up in the boat. Was he not surrounded by his favorite food? After all, their boat was carved from manioc root! He couldn't help himself—he gnawed a hole in the boat.

The noise woke Cat. "What was that?" she asked.

"It was just my stomach rumbling," said Rat. "Go back to sleep."

So Cat did, and Rat went right back to gnawing a hole in the boat.

The noise woke Cat again. "I know I heard something strange," she said.

"I think it was your stomach this time," said Rat. "Go back to sleep."

Cat fell asleep again, and this time Rat gnawed a hole right through the bottom of the boat. Water flowed in and soaked Cat's paws, and she jerked awake. She jumped up onto the side of the boat—cats don't like water, you know.

Then she saw the hole in the boat, and she knew what Rat had done. "You horrible Rat!" she cried.

"I was hungry! I couldn't help myself!" said Rat.

"I'm hungry, too!" said Cat. "Maybe I should eat *you*!" She leapt for Rat, but the boat overturned, and they both fell into the water.

They both swam and swam until finally they reached the shore. Cat was still angry. "I'm going to eat you!" she said again.

Rat shook water from his fur. "Yes, I deserve that," he said. "But at least wait until I dry off. I won't taste very good if I am all wet."

Cat thought he was right, so she set to licking herself dry and clean. She didn't notice Rat digging a hole.

Finally, when she thought Rat must be nice and dry, she turned around . . . just in time to see Rat jump into the hole, where she couldn't reach him!

"Come out!" cried Cat.

"No!" cried Rat. He dug deeper and deeper until finally he came out far away, where Cat couldn't find him.

From that day to this, Cat sleeps lightly so she will always hear when Rat is nearby. And Rat always runs from Cat, because he knows she will eat him if she can.

## 81  Five Saint Bernards

5 Saint Bernards in the Swiss Alps, looking for travelers in need of help.
1 followed a trail to an old cabin door, saved someone, and then there were 4.
4 Saint Bernards in the Swiss Alps, looking for travelers in need of help.
1 went to a forest of thick fir trees, saved someone, and then there were 3.
3 Saint Bernards in the Swiss Alps, looking for travelers in need of help.
1 followed the scent of stinky shoes, saved someone, and then there were 2.
2 Saint Bernards in the Swiss Alps, looking for travelers in need of help.
1 decided to go for a run, saved someone, and then there was 1.
1 Saint Bernard in the Swiss Alps, looking for travelers in need of help.
He found a traveler in the morning sun, then he went home because he was done.

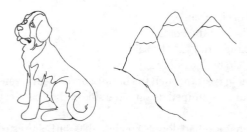

# Fingerplays and Songs

### 82 *¡Perros! ¡Perros! ¡Perros!* **A Rhyme in English and Spanish**

*¡Perros! ¡Perros! ¡Perros!* (PEH-roes)
Dogs! Dogs! Dogs!

*Perros arriba, perros abajo, perros todas partes*
(PEH-roes ar-REE-bah, PEH-roes ah-BAH-ho, PEH-roes TOH-das PAR-tes).
Dogs up, dogs down, dogs all around.

*Perros grandes, perros pequeños, perros entre*
(PEH-roes GRAHN-des, PEH-roes peh-KEH-nyos, PEH-roes en-TRAY).
Big dogs, little dogs, dogs in between.

*Perros sucios y perros limpios*
(PEH-roes SOO-seeose ee PEH-roes LEEM-peeose).
Dogs that are dirty and dogs that are clean.

*Perros mojados, perros temblor, perros secos*
(PEH-roes mo-HAH-dose, PEH-roes tem-BLORE, PEH-roes SEH-kohs).
Wet dogs, dogs shaking, dry dogs.

*Perros brincando* (PEH-roes breen-CAHN-doe).
Dogs jumping.

*Perros ladrando* (PEH-roes lah-DRAN-doe).
Dogs barking.

### 83 *Mon Chat Est Beau* (to the tune of "My Darling Clementine")

My kitty is so pretty, *(mime holding and petting kitty)*
The most beautiful I know.
And in French the way I say it is:
*Mon chat est beau* (mon SHOT ay BOW).

My kitty loves to dance, *(dance)*
He does a kitty dance just so.
And whenever I see him, I say:
*Mon chat est beau.*

When we go out to eat at *(mime eating)*
The little French bistro,
Everybody sees my kitty and knows
*Mon chat est beau.*

Then we come home to our *maison* (may-ZONE)
And it's off to bed we go.
And I dream about my kitty, because
*Mon chat est beau.*

## Crafts

### 84  Origami Cat

*Materials:* one 8-inch-square piece of origami paper or thin paper (not construction paper)

*Directions:*

1. Hold the paper so that it is in a diamond shape, and then fold it in half.
2. Fold each of the top two corners halfway down on each side.
3. Make a second fold on each side about one-half inch from the first fold.
4. Flip the point of each folded side up to make the cat ears.
5. Decorate as desired with eyes, nose, mouth, spots, and so on.

### 85  Origami Dog

*Materials:* one 8-inch-square piece of origami paper or thin paper (not construction paper)

*Directions:*

1. Hold the paper so that it is in a diamond shape, and then fold it in half.
2. Fold the corners down to make floppy dog ears.
3. Decorate as desired with eyes, nose, mouth, spots, and so on.

# 10 Clothes

## Books

**86  *Jamela's Dress* by Niki Daly. New York: Farrar, Straus and Giroux, 1999.**

A young South African girl gets so caught up in her excitement about the fabric her mother got for a new dress that she doesn't realize she is ruining it. With help from her friends, though, everything works out. This story incorporates the sights, sounds, and language of South Africa into a satisfying family tale. After reading, ask the children where they normally get their clothes, and if any of them have ever had clothes made especially for them.

**87  *Nabeel's New Pants: An Eid Tale* by Fawzia Gilani-Williams. Tarrytown, NY: Marshall Cavendish, 2007.**

Nabeel, a shoemaker in Turkey, buys gifts for his family for Eid, the celebration that ends Ramadan. He also buys a new pair of pants for himself, but finds they are too long. Neither his wife nor his mother nor his daughter has time to hem them for him, so he does it himself. Complications arise when his family members each stop by and hem the pants after all—leaving him with shorts!

**88  *Mama's Saris* by Pooja Makhijani. New York: Little, Brown, 2007.**

When a little girl celebrates her seventh birthday, she insists that she is old enough to wear saris like her mother does. As one sari after another is unpacked, the girl settles on a blue one that makes her feel not only grown up but as beautiful as her mother.

89   *What Can You Do with a Rebozo?* by Carmen Tafolla. Berkeley, CA:
Tricycle Press, 2008.

A family shows the many ways a rebozo, a traditional Mexican shawl, can be used. Read the author's note about rebozos in the back of the book. Ask the children to suggest the silliest, most creative, and most practical things they can think to do with a rebozo.

# Flannelboards

90   *Something Out of Nothing: A Jewish Folktale*

Joseph was a tailor. He could sew anything. One day he made himself a beautiful overcoat. He loved that overcoat. He wore it everywhere!

One day he tripped and fell, and the hem ripped. "Oh, no!" cried Joseph. "My overcoat is ruined!" Joseph thought for a bit, and then he got out his needle and thread. He snipped and cut and sewed, and made himself a jacket.

He loved that jacket. He wore it everywhere!

One day he bent his arm, and his elbow went right through the sleeve. "Oh, no!" cried Joseph. "My jacket is ruined!" Joseph thought for a bit, and then he got out his needle and thread. He snipped and cut and sewed, and made himself a vest.

He loved that vest. He wore it everywhere!

One day he was eating some soup, and it dripped down on his vest. "Oh, no!" cried Joseph. "My vest is ruined!" Joseph thought for a bit, and then he got out his needle and thread. He snipped and cut and sewed, and made himself a necktie.

He loved that necktie. He wore it everywhere!

One day he spilled juice right down on his tie and stained it. "Oh, no!" cried Joseph. "My necktie is ruined!" Joseph thought for a bit, and then he got out his needle and thread. He snipped and cut and sewed, and made himself a handkerchief.

He loved that handkerchief. He wore it everywhere!

One day he got his handkerchief out to blow his nose, and he saw that there was a hole right in the middle of it. "Oh, no!" cried Joseph. "My handkerchief is ruined!" Joseph thought for a bit, and then he got out his needle and thread. He snipped and cut and sewed, and found he had just enough clean fabric left to cover a button.

He used that button on his suspenders. He loved that button. He wore it everywhere!

One day he went to attach his suspenders, and his button was gone. "Oh, no!" cried Joseph. "My button is gone! What will I do? Even I, Joseph the Tailor, cannot make something out of nothing." Then he thought for a moment, and he said, "A-ha! I know! There is just enough left to make a story!" And that is what you have just heard!

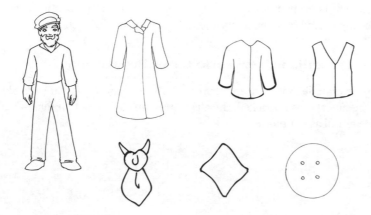

**91** *The Girl Who Wore Too Much: A Folktale from Thailand* by Margaret Read MacDonald. Little Rock, AR: August House, 1998.

A spoiled young girl can't decide which of her beautiful clothes and jewels to wear to the dance, and so she wears them all. But she is so weighted down that she can't get to the dance! To tell this story as a flannelboard, create the girl and multiple sets of clothing using felt so that you can layer them on the figure of the girl. You could also tell this as a prop story, layering clothing and jewels on yourself or a volunteer helper.

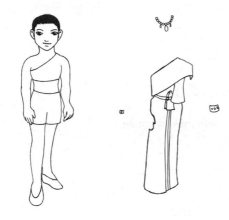

# Fingerplays and Songs

**92** *Chaleco* (cha-LAY-koe)**: A Guessing Rhyme**

In the mountains of Peru (*lift arms to create mountain shape*)
I wear my bright *chaleco*. (*indicate clothes*)
I pull it on like this each day (*mime pulling vest on*)
And on my way I go!

It has no sleeves, but keeps me warm (*place hands at shoulders, where vest cuts off*)
As I work or play or rest.
It only comes down to my waist. (*place hands at waist*)
My *chaleco* is a . . . (vest)!

**93 Dress Up** (to the tune of "Here We Go 'Round the Mulberry Bush")

Today's a day to get dressed up, get dressed up, get dressed up,
Today's a day to get dressed up, and play make believe.

I think I'll wear a Japanese kimono, Japanese kimono, Japanese kimono,
I think I'll wear a Japanese kimono and fly kites at the festival.

I think I'll wear shiny boots, shiny boots, shiny boots,
I think I'll wear shiny boots, to dance the samba at the Brazilian Carnival.

I think I'll wear a large headdress, a large headdress, a large headdress,
I think I'll wear a large headdress and dance in Zambia's harvest festival.

I think I'll wear a crown of flowers, a crown of flowers, a crown of flowers,
I think I'll wear a crown of flowers and dance around the May Pole.

# Craft

### 94 **Peruvian _Chaleco_**

Make a colorful vest like those worn by the people of the Andes.

*Materials:* a brown paper shopping bag, scissors, hole punch, two 6-inch pieces of yarn, crayons or markers

*Directions:*

1. Turn the bag upside down.
2. Cut out holes for the head and arms.
3. Cut a vertical slit from the head hole to the edge of the bag. This will be the chest opening.
4. Decorate the bag with colorful designs.
5. Cut 1-inch slits along the bottom edge of the vest to make a fringe.
6. Punch a hole on each side of the front opening.
7. Tie a piece of yarn to each hole.
8. Put the vest on and tie the yarn pieces together to hold it closed.

# 11
# Community Helpers

## Books

**95** ***Tito, the Firefighter / Tito, el bombero* by Tim Hoppey. Green Bay, WI: Raven Tree, 2004.**

Tito admires the *bomberos*, the firefighters, in his neighborhood. One day his ability to speak Spanish allows him to help them and become an honorary *bombero*. The simple text incorporates basic Spanish words.

**96** ***Beatrice's Goat* by Page McBrier. New York: Atheneum, 2001.**

When Beatrice's family in Uganda receives a goat from Heifer International, Beatrice finds tending the goat and selling the goat's milk provides her enough money to go to school.

**97** ***My Librarian Is a Camel* by Margriet Ruurs. Honesdale, PA: Boyds Mills Press, 2005.**

When we think of libraries, we think of buildings that have shelves and shelves of books, with librarians helping people. But you would be surprised to find that different countries have unique ways of providing books and library services for their communities.

**98** ***Crepes by Suzette* by Monica Wellington. New York: Dutton, 2004.**

Suzette works her way through Paris selling crepes from her cart each day. After reading the story, share the author's note discussing the Paris landmarks and artists featured in the story.

# Flannelboard

### 99  Community Helpers

Teach the children the following Spanish words, and then ask the questions below. Encourage the children to answer in Spanish.

> firefighter: *bombero* (bom-BEH-roe)
> police officer: *policía* (poe-lee-SEE-ah)
> doctor: *médico* (MEH-dee-co)
> trash collector: *basurero* (bah-soo-REH-roe)
> teacher: *professor* (pro-feh-SORE)

Help! There's a fire! Who do I call?
Help! Someone stole my bike! Who do I call?
Help! I broke my leg! Who do I call?
Help! My trash is overflowing! Who do I call?
Help! I need to learn to read! Who do I call?

# Fingerplays and Songs

### 100  Himalayan Sherpa

When climbing to Mount Everest, (*pretend to climb*)
The tallest mountain peak,
Ask for the guidance of a Sherpa,
He'll have all the answers you seek.

Sherpas are skilled mountaineers,
They'll guide you to the top.
They also know when it's too dangerous,
And tell you when to stop. (*put your hand out to signal stop*)

Sherpas make sure you're dressed
In special mountain climbing gear. (*pretend to tie shoes*)
They also know when it's safest to climb,
And which months to avoid during the year.

If your pack's too heavy,
Don't fret or worry a bit.
Sherpas will add it to their load,
Making sure everything fits. (*walk in place bent over, pretending to carry a heavy pack*)

When you reach the peak
And are admiring the view,
Remember to thank the Sherpa
Who helped guide you.
*Thank you!*

## 101 *The Mailman: A Traditional Czech Rhyme

Mailman, mailman, who are you looking for?
Mailman, are you looking for me?
Blow your horn loud and clear,
That's what I want to hear.
I hope you brought a letter for me!

## 102 *The People in My Neighborhood: A Song in ASL and English
(to the tune of "The Wheels on the Bus")

The people in my neighborhood help me out, help me out, help me out.
The people in my neighborhood help me out, all through my life.
The POLICE officer in my neighborhood keeps me safe . . .
The FIREFIGHTER in my neighborhood puts out fires . . .
The CONSTRUCTION WORKER in my neighborhood builds our houses . . .
The LETTER CARRIER in my neighborhood brings my mail . . .
The TEACHER in my neighborhood helps me learn . . .
The LIBRARIAN in my neighborhood helps me find books . . .

**103** **"Chez Paris"** from *Ratatouille: What's Cooking.* Burbank, CA: Walt Disney Records, 2007.

This fun tune describes many of the specialty foods and people found in a café in Paris. Dance around with shaker eggs to the music!

# Craft

**104** **Community Helpers ASL Matching Game**

*Materials:* community helpers worksheet (from website), ASL graphics (from website), glue, crayons or markers

*Directions:*

1. Glue the ASL graphics into the space under the pictures of the community helpers they match.
2. Color the paper as desired.

Match the correct hat and sign to each community helper.

# 12
# Counting

· · · · · · · · · · · · · · · · · · · · · · · · · · · · · · · · · · · · · · ·

## Books

**105** *Can You Count Ten Toes? Count to 10 in 10 Different Languages* by **Lezlie Evans. Boston: Houghton Mifflin, 1999.**

A cat travels the world, learning to count to ten in Japanese, Russian, Korean, Zulu, French, Hindi, Tagalog, Hebrew, Spanish, and Chinese. Pronunciation notes are included for each word.

**106** *\*Island Counting 1 2 3* by Frané Lessac. Cambridge, MA: Candlewick, **2005.**

From one little island to ten children celebrating carnival, this simple Caribbean counting book is bold and bright.

**107** *How Many Donkeys? An Arabic Counting Tale* by Margaret Read **MacDonald and Nadia Jameel Taibah. Morton Grove, IL: Whitman, 2009.**

Silly Jouha is taking his donkeys to market, and he constantly has to recount them—each time he is riding a donkey he forgets to count that one, and so he thinks he has lost one. The book features counting from one to ten in Arabic.

**108** *\*One Is a Drummer* by Roseanne Thong. San Francisco: Chronicle, 2004.

A group of children count to ten using various Chinese items. As you read the book, share the additional information about the objects in the back of the book.

# Flannelboards

### 109 *Just a Minute* by Yuyi Morales. San Francisco: Chronicle, 2004.

In this trickster tale with a Mexican flair, Grandma Beetle puts off the skeletal Señor Calavera ("skull" in Spanish) when he comes to take her away by involving him in the preparations for her birthday party.

### 110 *Count on Culebra: Go from 1 to 10 in Spanish* by Ann Whitford Paul. New York: Holiday House, 2008.

When Iguana hurts her toe, she's in too much pain to make her *dulces,* her cactus butter candies. But with help from Doctor Culebra ("snake"), she's soon too distracted with silliness to remember her pain.

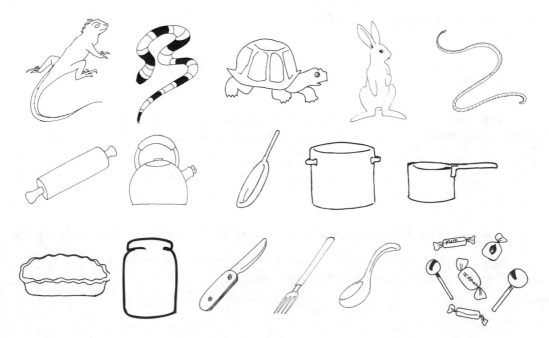

# Fingerplays and Songs

### 111  Ten Friends: An ASL Counting Rhyme

ONE is fun
But TWO is better.
THREE friends, FOUR friends
Play together.
FIVE friends are here now, and more!

Number SIX comes through the door.
Now SEVEN, EIGHT, and NINE, and then
Another friend comes in—it's TEN!
TEN good friends to run and play
And COUNT together every day!

**112** **"One Two Three"** from *Bridges Across the World: A Multicultural Songfest* **by Sarah Barchas. Sonoita, AZ: High Haven Music, 1999.**

This song teaches counting from one to three in English, Spanish, French, Italian, German, Russian, Chinese, Japanese, Korean, Vietnamese, Indonesian, and Swahili.

**113** **Head and Shoulders, Baby (in English and Chinese)**

Touch the indicated body parts as you sing the song.

Head and shoulders, baby, 1, 2, 3.
Head and shoulders, baby, 1, 2, 3.
Head and shoulders, head and shoulders,
Head and shoulders, baby, 1, 2, 3.

Shoulders, knees, baby, 1, 2, 3 . . .
Knees, toes, baby, 1, 2, 3 . . .

Complete the song once in English, and then teach the children how to count to three in Chinese. Repeat the song, replacing the English numbers with Chinese numbers.

> one: *yi* (YEE)
> two: *er* (ARR)
> three: *san* (SEN)

If you have an older group, you may even want to slowly incorporate more Chinese vocabulary until the children are singing the entire song in Chinese:

> baby: *wawa* (WA-wa)
> head: *tou* (TOE-ah)
> shoulder: *jian* (JEEN)
> knee: *xi* (SHEE)
> toe: *zhi* (ZHEE)

# Craft

**114** **Spanish Matching Counting Game**

*Materials:* worksheet (from website), crayons

*Directions:*

1. Draw a line to match the number to the picture showing that number of objects.
2. Color the picture as desired.

# Counting to Ten in Spanish

Draw a line to match each set of English and Spanish words
to the numbers they describe.

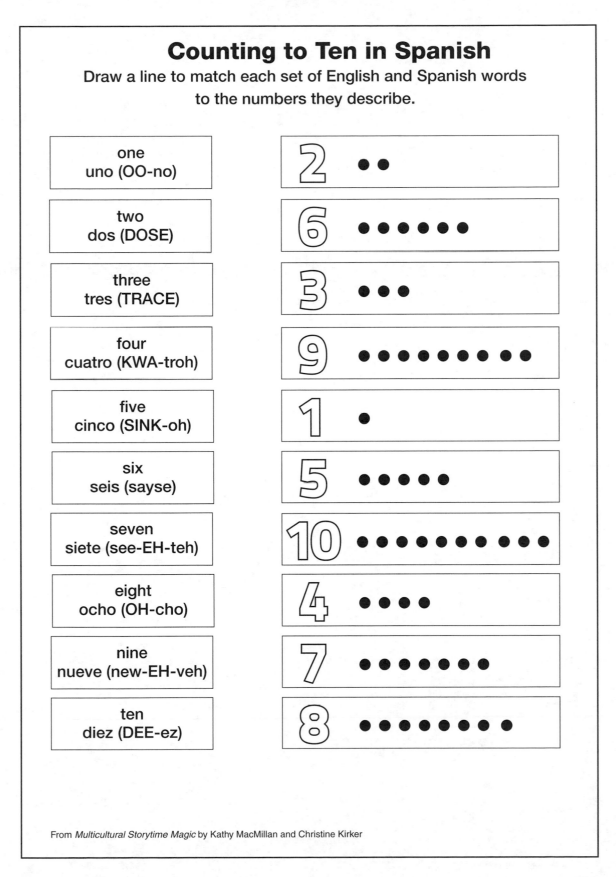

| one uno (OO-no) | 2 •• |
| two dos (DOSE) | 6 •••••• |
| three tres (TRACE) | 3 ••• |
| four cuatro (KWA-troh) | 9 ••••••••• |
| five cinco (SINK-oh) | 1 • |
| six seis (sayse) | 5 ••••• |
| seven siete (see-EH-teh) | 10 •••••••••• |
| eight ocho (OH-cho) | 4 •••• |
| nine nueve (new-EH-veh) | 7 ••••••• |
| ten diez (DEE-ez) | 8 •••••••• |

From *Multicultural Storytime Magic* by Kathy MacMillan and Christine Kirker

# 13
# Fairy Tales

## Books

**115** ***The Egyptian Cinderella* by Shirley Climo. New York: HarperCollins, 1989.**

Set in Egypt, this Cinderella story tells the tale of a Greek girl who is scorned by the Egyptian girls. However, when a falcon steals her rose-red gold slipper and delivers it to the Pharaoh, her life will be forever changed. After reading the story, discuss the similarities and differences between this version and the version the children are more familiar with.

**116** ***Pretty Salma: A Little Red Riding Hood Story from Africa* by Niki Daly. New York: Clarion, 2006.**

Set in Ghana, this story centers around Salma, who goes to the market for her granny carrying her big straw basket on her head and is tricked by Mr. Dog. Before reading the book, cover the references to Little Red Riding Hood on the cover and title page with paper and invite the children to guess which familiar fairy tale this story is most like. Then ask them to identify the ways the story is the same as and different from the traditional tale they know. (For a fun follow-up activity, see the Going to the Market activity from the "Shopping" chapter.)

**117** ***Glass Slipper, Gold Sandal: A Worldwide Cinderella* by Paul Fleischman. New York: Henry Holt, 2007.**

This clever retelling combines aspects of Cinderella stories from many lands, accompanied by illustrations that evoke the various cultures but still cohere in one book. This is a great discussion starter for comparing different versions of the same story, as it lays out the similar pieces of the story side by side. After reading, go through the story again and identify the different cultures and how the story differs in each.

118 ***The Three Little Tamales*** **by Eric A. Kimmel. Tarrytown, NY: Marshall Cavendish, 2009.**

In this adaptation of the story of the three little pigs, three tamales run away from the restaurant to avoid being eaten. But they haven't run far enough to escape Señor Lobo, the Big Bad Wolf. After reading, discuss how this story is the same as and different from the story of the three pigs.

# Flannelboards

### 119  The Magic Pomegranate: A Jewish Folktale

Adapted from the book by Peninnah Schram (Minneapolis, MN: Millbrook, 2008).

Long, long ago, there were three brothers. All three loved travel and adventure. They made a pact to go out into the world and have adventures, and then meet again ten years later, each bringing an unusual gift.

The oldest brother went west. He saw many amazing things: dancers, performers, magicians, and more. He saw a magician with a crystal ball. When the magician looked into the ball he could see the far reaches of the kingdom.

"I would like to buy that crystal ball from you," said the oldest brother. "I will take it with me when I meet my brothers, and it will be the most unusual gift."

The magician did not want to sell his crystal ball at first, but as the oldest brother offered more and more money, he finally gave in. The oldest brother paid the magician and tucked the ball under his arm.

The second brother went east. He was mesmerized by the markets and bazaars he saw, with each item more amazing than the next. At last he saw something so incredible he knew he had to buy it—it was a flying carpet. The second brother thought, "Surely this is the most unusual gift." He bought it on the spot.

The youngest brother went south. He saw beautiful forests full of colorful birds and lush trees and fruits. But one day he saw a tree more beautiful than any he had ever seen. It was a pomegranate tree. A pomegranate is a large red fruit full of delicious seeds. But this tree was strange—it was covered with beautiful orange-red blossoms, but only one fruit. The youngest brother reached for the pomegranate, and it fell into his hand. Before he could gasp in wonder, another pomegranate grew on the tree in its place. "Surely this is a magical pomegranate," he said. "I will take it to my brothers."

At the end of ten years, the three brothers reunited. They hugged one another and showed each other the unusual things they had found.

"Look at my crystal ball," said the oldest brother. "With it I can see places far away." He looked into the ball, and gasped. He saw, far away in another kingdom, a young princess lying ill, near death. "Brothers, we must help her!" he said.

"Here, climb onto my flying carpet and we shall go to her!" said the second brother. So the three brothers rode the flying carpet to the faraway kingdom where the princess lay.

The king of that country was heartbroken with grief for his daughter. Every doctor in the land had tried to cure her, but none could. At last the king sent out a message: "Anyone who can save my daughter will earn her hand in marriage."

When the three brothers arrived and heard the message, the youngest brother knew that his magical pomegranate could help. So he stepped forward and offered the pomegranate to the princess. He cut it open and fed her the juicy red kernels.

In just a few moments, the princess's pale cheeks began to grow pink and healthy. She sat up and laughed. The magical pomegranate had cured her!

The king was overjoyed. "The man who saved my daughter will marry her," he said.

But the brothers quarreled. "If I had not seen her in my crystal ball, we wouldn't even have known she was ill!" said the oldest brother.

"Ah, but without my flying carpet, we could not have come here!" said the second brother.

"Without my magical pomegranate, we could not have cured her," said the third brother quietly.

The king was not sure what to do. He looked at his daughter, whom he knew was very wise, and said, "Daughter, which man would you marry?"

The princess looked at the three brothers. "The crystal ball and the flying carpet are now as they ever were. But the youngest brother had to give up part of his pomegranate to cure me. He has performed the greatest good deed, because he had to give something up to do it."

And so the princess married the youngest brother and became her father's wisest advisor. When it came her time to rule the kingdom, she and the youngest brother ruled with wisdom and kindness all the days of their lives.

**120** **"The Little Rooster and the Heavenly Dragon" from *Celebrate the World: Twenty Tellable Folktales for Multicultural Festivals* by Margaret Read MacDonald. New York: H. W. Wilson, 1994.**

In this folktale from China, Little Rooster loans his horns to the devious Heavenly Dragon and loses them forever.

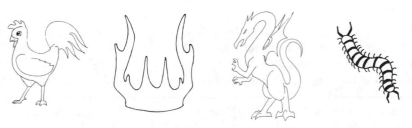

# Fingerplays and Songs

### 121 Old King Cole: An English Nursery Rhyme (adapted traditional)

Old King Cole was a merry old soul, and a merry old soul was he.
He called for his pipe in the middle of the night,
And he called for his fiddlers three.

Every fiddler had a fine fiddle, and a very fine fiddle had he.
Oh there's none so rare as can compare
With King Cole and his fiddlers three.

Old King Cole was a merry old soul, and a merry old soul was he.
He jumped for his pipe in the middle of the night, (*have children jump up and down*)
And he jumped for his fiddlers three!

Old King Cole was a merry old soul, and a merry old soul was he.
He turned for his pipe in the middle of the night, (*have children turn around*)
And he turned for his fiddlers three!

Old King Cole was a merry old soul, and a merry old soul was he.
He skipped for his pipe in the middle of the night, (*have children skip*)
And he skipped for his fiddlers three!

Old King Cole was a merry old soul, and a merry old soul was he.
He hopped for his pipe in the middle of the night, (*have children hop*)
And he hopped for his fiddlers three!

Old King Cole was a merry old soul, and a merry old soul was he.
He ran for his pipe in the middle of the night, (*have children run in place*)
And he ran for his fiddlers three!

### 122 Create a Mixed-Up Fairy Tale

This silly story combines elements from fairy tales around the world. Begin by explaining to the children that they will make their own silly story. Read the four choices in each set of parentheses and let the children select one item from each set. If your group is small enough, let each child choose one. For larger groups, have the children vote by a show of hands. Underline their choices, and then read back the completed, silly story.

Once upon a time there was a (happy/silly/pretty/small) (boy/girl/kangaroo/dog) named (Marie/Pedro/Salma/Cho). (She/He) lived in a (small/big/faraway/crowded) town called (Paris/Moscow/Beijing/New York). Everyone (loved/smiled at/was scared of/was angry at) (her/him) because (she/he) was so (beautiful/tall/friendly/silly). But what (she/he) wanted most in the world was (a pet/a magic wand/a crown/a talking frog).

One day, (she/he) set out for the (palace/market/library/countryside). But along the way, (she/he) met a (fox/coyote/bee/koala). This animal was very (sad/friendly/angry/talkative). It said, "Give me your (lunch/jacket/shoe/book) and I will let you pass." (Character's name) started to (run/cry/shout/wave her/his arms). The animal shouted, "Please (stop/run/come here/go away)!"

Just then, who should come along but the (king/queen/emperor/raja). (She/He) said, "(Animal's name), stop that right now." But the animal didn't listen.

Then, a (mermaid/witch/magical crocodile/dragon) showed up with (a crystal ball/a magic wand/an enchanted rose/a talking frog). The animal became (scared/excited/grumpy/friendly) and (ran away/swam away/disappeared/hugged everyone). "Good," said (Character's name). "Now we can all (live/jump/run/dance) (happily/sadly/crazily/sleepily) ever after."

**123 Magic Harp Singing Game**

In the English fairy tale "Jack and the Beanstalk," Jack steals a magic harp from the giant's castle. In this game you will invite the children to become magic harps themselves.

1. Cut a giant arrow out of cardboard. If desired, decorate your arrow with fairy tale designs.
2. Select a simple song that everyone knows, such as "Row, Row, Row, Your Boat" or "Mary Had a Little Lamb."
3. As the group begins to sing together, move your arrow up and down to control their volume. When the arrow is pointing straight out to the side, they should sing at medium volume. When the arrow is pointing straight up, they should sing as loudly as possible. When the arrow is pointing straight down, they should only mouth the words.

# Craft

**124 Fleur-de-Lis Shield**

For many years, the fleur-de-lis, a stylized lily or iris, was used as a symbol of France's royalty. It is still used in many popular designs today.

*Materials:* shield shape cut from posterboard, fleur-de-lis (from website), yarn, markers, colored pencils or crayons, scissors, hole punch

*Directions:*

1. Glue the fleur-de-lis shape onto the shield.
2. Using markers, crayons, or colored pencils, decorate the shield as desired.
3. Punch holes in the top sides (shoulder area) of the shield.
4. Tie yarn to each hole and slip the shield over your head.

# 14
# Fall

• • • • • • • • • • • • • • • • • • • • • • • • • • • • • • • • • • • • • • • •

## Books

**125  *One Child, One Seed: A South African Counting Book* by Kathryn Cave. New York: Henry Holt, 2002.**

A South African girl named Nothando plants a pumpkin in this beautifully photo-illustrated picture book. The story is actually three books in one: on the left-hand side of each spread is simple text that offers a basic counting story—just enough for a toddler audience. For preschoolers, librarians can read the extended story in the middle of the page. For older readers, a sidebar on the right offers more cultural background to the story. Each through line is a complete read-aloud unto itself, or two or more parts can be combined if desired.

**126  *The Autumn Equinox: Celebrating the Harvest* by Ellen Jackson. Brookfield, CT: Millbrook, 2000.**

This book discusses how various countries throughout the world celebrate and prepare for the fall harvest.

**127  *In the Leaves* by Huy Voun Lee. New York: Henry Holt, 2005.**

Xiao Ming and his mother spend the day among the turning leaves of autumn, and he learns the Chinese characters for the things they see. This book does an excellent job of showing how Chinese characters represent concepts through pictures. Explain that our alphabet represents sounds, while in Chinese writing, each symbol represents an idea. For a fun follow-up activity, copy and enlarge the symbols and illustrations from the endpapers of the book. Mix up the pictures and see if the children can match each picture to the symbol that goes with it.

128 ***Thanking the Moon: Celebrating the Mid-Autumn Moon Festival* by Grace Lin. New York: Knopf, 2010.**

Each member of a Chinese family adds an item to the celebration of the Mid-Autumn Moon Festival. This book includes an author's note explaining the festival's customs and traditions.

# Flannelboards

### 129 The Colors of Fall

Using the template, cut out leaves of red, yellow, green, and brown. Use the leaves to introduce the Spanish words for the colors, and then share the guessing game rhyme with the children to reinforce the color vocabulary.

*Spanish pronunciation:*

red: *rojo* (ROH-ho)
yellow: *amarillo* (ah-mah-REE-yo)
green: *verde* (VAIR-deh)
brown: *café* (cah-FEH)
What color is it?: *De qué color es?* (de keh co-LORE ess)

When leaves of this color hang on the tree,
They look like apples to me. *De qué color es?* (*rojo*)
When leaves of this color hang on the tree,
They look like little suns to me. *De qué color es?* (*amarillo*)
When leaves of this color hang on the tree,
They look like blades of grass to me. *De qué color es?* (*verde*)
When leaves of this color hang on the tree,
They look like chocolate cookies to me. *De qué color es?* (*café*)

### 130 "The Pumpkin Child" from *Celebrate the World: Twenty Tellable Folktales for Multicultural Festivals* by Margaret Read MacDonald. New York: H. W. Wilson, 1994.

In this Iranian folktale, an old woman prays for a child and receives a little pumpkin child who grows up to marry the prince.

# Fingerplays and Songs

### 131  A Harvest Gift

This rhyme is based on a Slovakian harvest tradition in which a single shock of wheat is left standing in the field when all the others have been stored away in the barn for the winter. This shock, called a *boroda* ("beard"), is tied with ribbon and left as a gift for the field mice so that they will stay out of the barn.

Harvest time is here,
We gather all the wheat (*mime gathering wheat*)
And tie it into bundles (*mime tying bow*)
Stacked nice and neat. (*point to stacks of wheat*)

Carry them into the barn (*mime carrying bundle of wheat*)
To save for winter's cold. (*shiver*)
But we'll leave one shock standing (*hold hands parallel to each other
    and raise from floor to chest height*)
So lovely to behold.

We'll tie it up with ribbon (*mime tying ribbon*)
And leave it as a gift
For our little field mice friends (*hold hands close to face like a mouse's paws*)
With long tails and noses swift. (*twitch nose*)

Eat up, eat up, our field mice friends! (*mime eating*)
And stay out of our barn. (*shake finger*)
Enjoy this wheat all winter long (*shiver*)
Till spring comes, nice and warm. (*raise hands over head to make sun*)

### 132  Peep Squirrel: A Playsong from the African American Tradition (adapted traditional)

This song is traditionally used as part of a chase game in which the children line up and one child (the "squirrel") weaves in and out among them until the "catch that squirrel" verse, when the other children try to tag the squirrel and take over his or her role. If that's a little too wild for your storytime, try this action-in-place version instead. Invite the children to begin by crouching down and pretending to be squirrels, then acting out the words as you sing them. You can hear the tune for this song on *Shake It to the One That You Love Best: Play Songs* and *Lullabies from Black Musical Traditions* by Cheryl Warren Mattox (El Sobrante, CA: Warren-Mattox Productions, 1989).

Peep, squirrel, yadda-deeda-didda-dum.
Peep, squirrel, yadda-deeda-didda-dum.

Jump, squirrel . . .
Run, squirrel . . .
Hide, squirrel . . .
Peep, squirrel . . .
Hop, squirrel . . .
Scurry, squirrel . . .
Yawn, squirrel . . .
Sleep, squirrel . . .

# Craft

### 133 Pumpkin Lantern

Cultures around the world celebrate the abundance of the harvest with festivals of thanksgiving. Many cultures also use lanterns in their festivals to represent the longer nights.

*Materials:* paper bowl, black construction paper, yellow tissue paper, crayons, glue, scissors

*Directions:*

1. Cut eye and mouth shapes from the bottom of the bowl.
2. Place yellow tissue paper in the bowl to give the illusion of a glowing lit lantern.
3. Decorate the bowl as desired.
4. Glue the edge of the bowl to the black construction paper. Decorate as desired. Children can use yellow crayons to show the glow of light on black paper.

# 15
# Family

## Books

**134** *Carolina's Gift: A Story of Peru* **by Katacha Diaz. Norwalk, CT: Soundprints, 2002.**

Carolina and her mother visit the Sunday market to find the perfect birthday gift for Carolina's *abuelita* ("grandmother"). After perusing the pretty hats, birds, and other wonders, Carolina settles on a walking stick—so Abuelita can come with them to market the following week.

**135** *Luka's Quilt* **by Georgia Guback. New York: Greenwillow, 1994.**

Luka, a young Hawaiian girl, has a close relationship with her grandmother, Tutu. When Tutu makes her a traditional Hawaiian quilt, Luka is disappointed that it has only two colors instead of the colorful flowers she had envisioned, and Tutu is disappointed that Luka doesn't like the quilt she worked so hard to make. On Lei Day, they declare a truce and attend the festival together, and things get better when they begin to understand each other's point of view. Though the story is steeped in Hawaiian culture, its emotional reality is universal.

**136** *\*The World Turns Round and Round* **by Nicki Weiss. New York: Greenwillow, 2000.**

Children around the world receive gifts of clothing from their grandmothers. The rhyming text features simple clothing and family vocabulary in Spanish, Swahili, Japanese, Russian, Hindi, Arabic, Vietnamese, and French.

**137** *Yoko's Paper Cranes* **by Rosemary Wells. New York: Hyperion, 2001.**

When Yoko moves from Japan to California, she finds a special way to send birthday wishes back to Obaasan, her grandmother. After reading the story, make origami cranes like Yoko does. Simple directions can be found at www.operationmigration.org/Origami.pdf.

## Flannelboard

### 138 What Does Baby Want? A Flannelboard Story in English and French

*Bébé* (beh-beh) ("baby") was crying, wah wah wah.
*Frère* (frair) ("brother") came along and said, "A-ha!
I know what to do, and it is this."
He picked up that *bébé* and gave her a kiss!
And the *bébé* laughed!
But then . . .

Repeat with:

> sister: *soeur* (sir)
> grandmother: *grand-mère* (grand-mair)
> grandfather: *grand-père* (grand-pair)
> mother: *mère* (mair)
> father: *père* (pair)

*Bébé* was crying, wah wah wah.
The whole *famille* (fa-MEE-ya) said, "A-ha!
We know what to do, and it is this."
They all hugged that *bébé* and gave her a kiss!
And the *bébé* laughed, and smiled, and cuddled up . . . and went to sleep!

## Fingerplays and Songs

### 139 *One Is Daddy: A Rhyme from the Czech Republic

Starting with the index finger, touch each finger in turn as you say the rhyme.

1 is Daddy,
2 is Mommy,
3 is Grandpa,
4 is Grandma,
And little number 5 is the grandson.

**140  Family Simon Says**

Mexican families look just like our own. They are made up of:

mother: *madre* (MAH-dreh)
father: padre (PAH-dreh)
brother: hermano (air-MAH-no)
sister: hermana (air-MAH-nah)
grandmother: abuela (ah-BWAY-la)
grandfather: abuelo (ah-BWAY-low)

Play a form of Simon Says. If the *madre*, *padre*, *abuela*, or *abuelo* gives directions, the children should follow them (for example, "*Madre* says touch your toes!"). If the *hermano* or *hermana* gives directions, the children should not follow them (for example, "*Hermano* says jump up and down!").

**141  *Family Song: A Song in ASL and English** (to the tune of "My Darling Clementine")

I've got a mommy (MOTHER), got a daddy (FATHER).
Got a SISTER and a BROTHER.
All together we're a FAMILY,
And we all LOVE one another.

**142  Uncle John: A Song from Hungary** (to the tune of "Frère Jacques")

Sing the song, and then ask the children if they know another song that is similar to it. They will likely know it as "Are You Sleeping?" Explain that this song is one that children around the world sing, and the words change to fit different cultures and languages.

Uncle John, Uncle John,
Wake up, wake up!
They chime the bells,
They call for lunch,
Ding dang dong.
Ding dang dong.

# Craft

### 143  Scottish Tartan Weaving

In Scotland, which is now part of Great Britain, weavers traditionally made bright plaid fabrics for people to wear. Each weaver used a different design, with different colors depending on where he lived and which plants were available to use for dyes. People lived in extended family groupings called clans, and because each clan generally had one weaver who made a certain design, that design came to represent the clan. In this craft, the children will design and create their own tartan for their family! As they choose the colors for their tartan, ask them to think about where they live and the things that are important to them.

*Materials:* construction paper in various colors, tape

*Directions:*

1. Cut construction paper into strips of various thicknesses, 8–10 strips per child.
2. For the base, fold a piece of construction paper in half. Cut slits about an inch apart, beginning from the folded side of the paper and stopping about one inch from the edge. Unfold the paper. (These first two steps may be done ahead of time.)
3. Weave each strip through the slits in the paper, over and under, to make a beautiful design.
4. Each time you finish a row, push it up to the top.
5. When you are finished, fold the ends of the strips around to the back of the paper and tape them down.

# 16
# Farm Fun

## Books

**144  *Why Ducks Sleep on One Leg* by Sherry Garland. New York: Scholastic, 1993.**

In this pourquoi tale from Vietnam, three ducks who were created with only one leg each attempt to petition the Jade Emperor for additional legs, but end up with a creative solution to their problems.

**145  *The Bossy Gallito* by Lucia M. Gonzalez. New York: Scholastic, 1994.**

In this traditional Cuban folktale, a bossy rooster tells everybody what to do, but they all refuse until his friend the sun agrees to help him.

**146  \*The Farmyard Jamboree* by Margaret Read MacDonald. Cambridge, MA: Barefoot Books, 2005.**

This cumulative story, inspired by a Chilean folktale, features repetition and makes for excellent audience participation. This story could also be made into a flannelboard, stick puppet, or prop story.

**147  *Little Rooster's Diamond Button* by Margaret Read MacDonald. Morton Grove, IL: Whitman, 2007.**

When Little Rooster finds a diamond button on the road, the king tries to take it from him. But with a little help from his magic stomach, the rooster foils the king's plans, with hilarious results! This Hungarian folktale is always a hit with kids.

# Flannelboards

### 148  *Borreguita and the Coyote* by Verna Aardema. New York: Knopf, 1991.

Clever Borreguita (Spanish for "little lamb") outsmarts the coyote again and again in this Mexican folktale. Use a spray bottle of water to provide the splash when the rock goes into the water. This story could also be presented as a stick puppet story:

1. Create stick puppets using the sheep and coyote templates.
2. Cut the pond shape out of cardboard, and then cover it with tinfoil.
3. Cut two identical circles from yellow construction paper for the moon and its reflection.
4. Use a potted plant for the clover patch.
5. Use a real rock and a spray bottle of water for the splash.

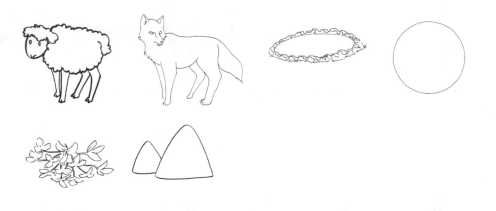

### 149  *When I First Came to This Land* by Harriet Ziefert. New York: Putnam, 1998.

This cumulative verse, based on a German immigrant song, tells the story of a man who came to America and gradually built a farm and a life for himself. Kids will enjoy joining in to repeat the silly names of the animals and parts of the farm. For large groups, print, color, and laminate multiple copies of each illustration, then attach craft sticks to the backs. Pass one piece out to each child, and have the children hold the items up during their part of the story.

# Fingerplays and Songs

### 150  **Down on Grandpa's Farm** (traditional)

Using pictures, introduce the Spanish vocabulary for the following farm animals:

> cow: *vaca* (VAH-cah)
> piglet: *cerdito* (ser-DEE-toe)
> sheep: *oveja* (oh-VEH-hah)
> duck: *pato* (PAH-toe)
> dog: *perro* (PEH-roe)
> horse: *caballo* (cah-BAHL-yo)

Down on Grandpa's farm there is a big brown *vaca*.
Down on Grandpa's farm there is a big brown *vaca*.
The *vaca*, she makes a sound like this: moo moo!
The *vaca*, she makes a sound like this: moo moo!

Repeat with other animals.

### 151  **What Does the Animal Say?**

As you share the following rhyme, ask the children to guess what each animal is by its sound. Explain that, in Japanese, animal sounds are pronounced differently than they are in English.

Let's visit a farm in Japan today.
What do you think the animals will say?
This animal says "*wan-wan*." Can you guess what it is? (dog)

. . . *mee-mee* (sheep)
. . . *qua-qua* (duck)
. . . *boo* (pig)
. . . *neeow* (cat)
. . . *qui-qui* (bird)
. . . *he-heeh* (horse)
. . . *mo-mo* (cow)

### 152  *****The Cow: A Traditional Chinese Nursery Rhyme**

A cow is on the mountain.
The old saying goes,
On her legs are four feet,
On her feet are eight toes.
Her tail is behind
On the end of her back,
And her head is in front
On the end of her neck.

### 153  *****"Ride, Horse, Ride" from *I Have a Dream: World Music for Children* by Daria Marmaluk-Hajioannou. Riegelsville, PA: Dariamusic, 2009.**

This Native American song expresses respect for all animals, including horses, and appreciation for all that horses can do for people. Dance with rhythm sticks or drums to the song.

# Craft

### 154  Farm Animals Spanish Matching Game

*Materials:* Spanish Farm Animals worksheet (from website), crayons

*Directions:*

1. Draw a line to match the English and Spanish words to the correct pictures.
2. Color as desired.

# Animals on the Farm

Draw a line to match the English and Spanish words
with the animals they describe.

duck
pato (PAH-toe)

cow
vaca (VAH-cah)

dog
perro (PEH-roe)

piglet
cerdito (ser-DEE-toe)

horse
caballo (cah-BAHL-yo)

sheep
oveja (oh-VEH-hah)

From *Multicultural Storytime Magic* by Kathy MacMillan and Christine Kirker

# 17
# Fast and Slow

## Books

**155  *All the Way to Lhasa: A Tale from Tibet* by Barbara Helen Berger. New York: Philomel, 2002.**

This Tibetan variation on the theme of the tortoise and the hare finds a determined young boy reaching the holy city of Lhasa long before the hurrying horse and rider.

**156  *\*Turtle's Race with Beaver* by Joseph Bruchac. New York: Dial, 2003.**

In this retelling of a Seneca tale, Turtle spends the winter buried in the mud at the bottom of her pond, unaware that Beaver has moved in and created a dam and a lodge on the surface. When Turtle emerges and asks if they can share the pond, Beaver insists that they race, and the loser will have to leave. Turtle's cleverness and Beaver's temper ensure a win for Turtle and teach Beaver a lesson.

**157  *\*"Slowly, Slowly, Slowly," Said the Sloth* by Eric Carle. New York: Philomel, 2002.**

The animals of the Amazon rain forest question the sloth about his very slow habits.

**158  *The Hare and the Tortoise* by Helen Ward. Brookfield, CT: Millbrook, 1999.**

In this retelling of the traditional Aesop's fable, the tortoise still wins the race. Included are wonderful illustrations of animals from around the world who witnessed the race. The author includes notes on the various animals depicted in the book. After reading the story, use a map to show the children where the animals' homes are located.

# Flannelboard

### 159  The Water Buffalo and the Snail: A Folktale from the Philippines

Adapted from a story in *Philippine Folk Tales* by Mabel Cook Cole (Chicago: A. C. McClurg, 1916).

This story could also be told as a prop story. The group leader should use a buffalo puppet or mask and play the part of the water buffalo. Before telling the story, pass out shells or cutouts of snails to the children and ask them to play the part of the snail as you circle the room. Each time you call out "Snail!" point to a child, who should hold up his or her snail and say, "Here I am!"

One very hot day, a water buffalo went to the river to bathe. There he met a snail, and they began talking.

"You are very slow," said the water buffalo.

"Oh, no," replied the snail. "I can beat you in a race."

"Then let us try and see," said the water buffalo.

So they went out on the bank and started to run.

After the water buffalo had gone a long distance, he stopped and called, "Snail!"

And another snail lying by the river answered, "Here I am!"

Then the water buffalo, thinking that it was the same snail with which he was racing, ran on.

By and by he stopped again and called, "Snail!"

And another snail answered, "Here I am!"

The water buffalo was surprised that the snail could keep up with him. But he ran on and on, and every time he stopped to call, another snail answered him. And as far as I know, that water buffalo is still running today.

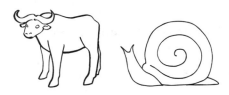

# Prop Story

### 160  *The Butterfly and the Crane: A Folktale from Fiji

Adapted from a story in *At Home in Fiji* by Constance Frederica Gordon Cumming (New York: A. C. Armstrong, 1883).

Make a simple butterfly puppet by folding a sheet of brightly colored tissue paper and securing it to a clothespin. Decorate with markers and glitter. To make the crane, cut out the shape from the template and decorate it, then cut along the center slit. Accordion-fold a square of white tissue paper and slide it into the slit to form the wings.

One day the butterfly told the crane about all the delicious shrimp he had seen in far-off Tonga. "I love shrimp!" said the crane.

"Then let us race!" said the butterfly.

"Race you? Why, you are just a teeny thing, and I am large and strong. I will surely win," said the crane.

"We shall see," said the butterfly.

They rose in the air and started off. After a while the crane looked back and said, "Ha! I cannot even see that silly little butterfly, he is so far behind me. I can rest and fly slowly now, without fear of his overtaking me."

But the butterfly was actually resting on the crane's back! When he heard the crane say this, he rose up and flew a little way ahead, calling, "Here I am, crane! Do hurry! I thought you were much faster than that."

The crane could not believe his eyes. He flapped his wings faster and sped ahead of the butterfly. The butterfly dropped onto the crane's back again, enjoying the ride as the crane sped through the air.

Again the crane looked back and said, "Ha! Now I have left him in the dust."

But the butterfly giggled and flew on ahead. He called, "Hurry, crane! We are nearly there."

"How did he get ahead of me again?" cried the crane. He flapped his wings even harder, though he was nearly dropping with exhaustion. The butterfly lit on the crane's back once more.

At last the crane landed in Tonga, many miles from where he had started. He was so tired that he lay on his back and covered his face with his wings.

The butterfly hopped into a nearby rock. "It's about time you got here," he said. "I've been waiting such a long time."

The crane stared at the butterfly in disbelief. "Never again will I call you slow and small, little butterfly," he said.

"Good," said the butterfly. "Now how about some shrimp?"

# Fingerplays and Songs

**161   In the South American Rain Forest**

I am a sloth, a two-toed sloth. (*sit down slowly*)
I sit in the trees all day.
I slowly eat buds and shoots and leaves, (*mime eating slowly*)
And slowly I walk away. (*walk slowly in place*)

I am a hummingbird, watch me fly! (*flap arms quickly*)
My wings beat extra fast.
Better look quickly when you hear me fly
Because soon I'll be racing past!

I am a snail, with my shell on my back,
And I inch along on the ground. (*crawl slowly on ground*)
I chew tiny plants with my tiny teeth.
Slow and steady's how I get around.

I am a jaguar, racing through the trees. (*run in place*)
Don't try to catch me—you'll fail!
I chase my prey in the sun all day.
I'm so fast all you'll see is my tail!

**162 Tingalayo** (adapted traditional)

If you are unfamiliar with this traditional Jamaican tune, you can find it on many children's CDs, including *The Best of Raffi* by Raffi (Toronto, ON: Universal, 2003). During the chorus, have the children gallop in a circle. During the verses, have them act out the words.

*Chorus:*

Tingalayo, come my little donkey, come.
Tingalayo, come my little donkey, come.

*Verses:*

My donkey jump,
My donkey leap,
My donkey kick with his two hind feet.
My donkey run,
He runs right past,
My donkey loves to run real fast!

Repeat chorus, galloping quickly.

My donkey hee,
My donkey haw,
My donkey rest in a bed of straw.
My donkey moan,
My donkey go,
But now he's tired so he goes real slow.

Repeat chorus, galloping slowly.

**163 "Fast and Slow" from *The Best of the Laurie Berkner Band*. New York: Two Tomatoes, 2010.**

This song, based on Aesop's fable of the tortoise and the hare, talks about the reasons why you would want to go slow and fast. Use with shakers or other instruments to show changes in rhythm.

# Craft

**164 *Turtle's Race with Beaver* Puppets**

*Materials:* turtle piece cut from green construction paper (from template on website), beaver face, body, and tail cut from brown construction paper (from template on website), spring-loaded clothespin, paper bag, glue, crayons

*Directions:*

1. Color the turtle and beaver as desired.
2. Glue the turtle to the clothespin so that the opening of the clothespin is under the turtle's mouth.
3. Glue the beaver face and body to a paper bag.
4. Glue the beaver tail to the back of the bag.
5. Retell *Turtle's Race with Beaver* using your puppets or make up a story of your own.

# 18
# Feelings

· · · · · · · · · · · · · · · · · · · · · · · · · · · · · · · · · · · · · · · · · · · · · · ·

## Books

**165** *Three Scoops and a Fig* **by Sara Akin. Atlanta: Peachtree, 2010.**

Sofia tries to help in the kitchen of her family's Italian restaurant, but is mortified when her mistakes cause her family to say she is too little. She can be proud, however, when she comes up with the perfect dessert for Nonna and Nonno, her grandparents, for their celebration supper.

**166** *Baboon* **by Kate Banks. New York: Farrar, Straus and Giroux, 1997.**

A young baboon explores the African grasslands with his mother. He draws conclusions about his surroundings based on what he senses. "The world is slow," he says after watching a turtle crawl by, but his mother encourages him to see the world in all its diversity.

**167** *Numero Uno* **by Alex Dorros and Arthur Dorros. New York: Abrams, 2007.**

Socrates is the smartest man in his Mexican village, and Hercules is the strongest. They constantly argue over which is more important—brains or brawn. Finally the villagers devise a contest, and the men are sent away for three days to see who will be most missed as the villagers build a bridge. With Spanish vocabulary sprinkled throughout, this silly story is made for storytimes.

**168** *\*So Happy!* **by Kevin Henkes. New York: Greenwillow, 2005.**

Set in the American Southwest, the brief text and engaging illustrations by Anita Lobel tell the interconnected stories of a boy, a seed, and a rabbit.

## Flannelboard

### 169 Anansi and the Fish Trap: An Ashanti Tale

Each time a feeling is mentioned in the story, pause and ask the children how someone might act if she or he felt that way. Encourage the children to act out each feeling as Bonsu does.

One day Anansi said, "I'm going to go fishing." Now, if you know anything about Anansi, you know that he hated hard work, and he loved to play tricks. So of course he was thinking about how he could get lots of fish without doing any work. "I know!" he said. "I'll find a partner, and I will trick him into doing all the work while I get all the fish!"

Now Anansi didn't know that his friend Bonsu was standing nearby and heard Anansi talking to himself. He knew all about the tricks Anansi had played in the past, and he decided to beat Anansi at his own game. So he walked right up to Anansi and said cheerfully, "Anansi! Would you like to go fishing with me today?"

"Ah!" thought Anansi. "Here is the fool I shall take as my partner."

"Certainly," Anansi said out loud. "Let's go down to the river."

On the way, Bonsu said, "Now, if we're going to be partners we need to split the work. Give me your knife and I will cut the branches to make a fish trap. Your part of the work will be to feel tired for me."

"Wait a minute!" cried Anansi. "Why should I do the hard part? I will cut the branches, and *you* feel tired."

So Anansi climbed the palm tree and started cutting the branches, and Bonsu sat nearby and cried, "Oh! I am so tired! Such weariness!"

When the branches were cut, Bonsu said, "Now I will make the trap. Your part can be to feel the misery of aching fingers and back."

"No!" said Anansi. "I will make the trap, and you feel the misery!"

So Anansi wove and tied the branches and made a fish trap. Bonsu sat nearby and grunted and groaned, rubbing his back and flexing his fingers.

They put the trap in the river. Immediately a fish swam into it. "Take this fish, Anansi," said Bonsu. "I will take whatever is in the trap in the morning."

Anansi looked at the fish, and said, "Oh, no. Surely there will be lots more fish in the morning. You take this fish now."

So Bonsu agreed and took the fish home and had a fine dinner with his wife.

The next morning when they went to the river and pulled the trap out, there was a snake in it! Bonsu stepped forward bravely. "I will pull the snake out, Anansi, and you feel scared for me."

"No!" said Anansi. "I will pull the snake out, and you feel the fear!"

So Anansi carefully lifted the snake out of the trap with a stick and tossed it away into the water, while Bonsu stood on the bank and chattered his teeth in fear, peering through his fingers.

Anansi looked into the fish trap. "The snake has eaten all the fish! This can't count as my turn. I will take whatever comes into the trap next. Let's wait and watch."

So Anansi and Bonsu put the trap back into the river and waited. Suddenly fish came leaping and swimming up the bank. Anansi clapped his hands in delight as they raced into the trap . . . but then he saw the crocodile that was chasing them! The crocodile swam right into the trap and then reared up in the water, wearing the trap on its head. It flailed about, smashing the fish trap in the process.

Finally the crocodile broke free and swam away. Anansi and Bonsu looked sadly at their ruined fish trap.

"I'm sorry," said Bonsu. "I will take the trap and sell it at the market, and you can feel ashamed for me at having such a worthless item to sell."

"No!" said Anansi. "I will sell the trap, and you can feel the shame." He grabbed the trap out of Bonsu's hand and marched straight to the market. But when the people at the market saw what a worthless trap Anansi had, they shouted at him, "How dare you insult us by bringing a ruined fish trap to sell! Do you think us idiots?"

And that was the end of Anansi's fishing business.

# Fingerplays and Songs

### 170  **How Do I Feel?**

I am *felíz* (feh-LEASE), you can tell by the big smile on my face.
What is *felíz*? (happy)

I am *enfadado* (en-fa-DA-doe), you can tell by the frown on my face.
What is *enfadado*? (angry)

I am *triste* (TREES-tay). I want to cry.
What is *triste*? (sad)

I am *tímido* (TEE-mee-doe), especially around strangers.
What is *tímido*? (shy)

### 171  **\* If You're Happy and You Know It** (adapted traditional)

If you're HAPPY and you know it, clap your hands.
If you're HAPPY and you know it, clap your hands.
If you're HAPPY and you know it, then your SIGNS will surely show it.
If you're HAPPY and you know it, clap your hands.

If you're SAD and you know it, cry some tears . . .
If you're SCARED and you know it, curl up into a ball . . .
If you're ANGRY and you know it, stomp your feet . . .
If you're EXCITED and you know it, jump up and down . . .

### 172 May There Always Be Sunshine: A Traditional Song from Russia

This song has been popularized by children's singer Jim Gill. You can find the tune on many of his albums, including *Jim Gill Sings the Sneezing Song and Other Contagious Tunes* (Chicago: Jim Gill Music, 1992). Introduce the traditional lyrics to the children, and then invite them to suggest things they love so much that they want them to always be. Write the list on a chalkboard or whiteboard, then sing the song again with their suggested items.

May there always be sunshine,
May there always be blue skies,
May there always be Mummy,
May there always be me!

# Craft

### 173 Worry Dolls

Children in Central America make small dolls called *worry dolls*. According to legend, if a child tells the doll her worries at night and places it under her pillow, by morning her worries will disappear.

*Materials:* round-head clothespin, various colors of yarn or embroidery floss, fine-tip marker, glue

*Directions:*

1. Wrap yarn or embroidery floss around the shaft of the clothespin. This is the body.
2. Using the marker, decorate the round head of the clothespin with eyes, a nose, and a mouth.
3. Cut pieces of yarn and glue them to the top for hair, or draw hair with markers.

# 19
# Food

## Books

**174 *Kallaloo! A Caribbean Tale* by David and Phillis Gershator. New York: Marshall Cavendish, 2005.**

A bouncy St. Thomas variation of "Stone Soup."

**175 *\*Bread Bread Bread* by Ann Morris. New York: HarperCollins, 1989.**

Simple text and color photos explore the different ways people make and eat bread around the world. The text emphasizes the commonalities, while the photos show the variety of breads in different cultures. A photo index identifies the locations of all the photos.

**176 *\*What Should I Make?* by Nandini Nayer. Toronto, ON: Tricycle Press, 2009.**

A little boy makes his own special *chapati*, an Indian flat bread, while his mother bakes some for the family. After reading the story, invite the children to discuss special foods that they make with their families.

**177 *Yoko* by Rosemary Wells. New York: Hyperion, 1998.**

Yoko, a Japanese American girl, loves to bring her favorite things—steamed rice and sushi—to school for lunch, but the other children think it's gross. Her teacher organizes an International Food Day to get the children to try new things, and though it's not the success she hopes, it does help Yoko find a friend.

# Flannelboard

### 178 Bee-Bim Bop

This flannelboard makes a great follow-up to *Bee-Bim Bop!* by Ho Baek Lee (New York: Clarion, 2004).

Give each child one of the ingredients in the traditional Korean dish bee-bim bop. As you say the rhyme, call out one of the ingredients and have the child holding that ingredient come up and add it to the pot, while the others pretend to stir.

Bee-bim bop, we'll mix it in our pot.
Let's add our garlic and stir it all up.

Continue until all ingredients have been added (onion, broccoli, spinach, peas, meat, eggs, rice, jalapeño peppers).

Bee-bim bop, we mixed it in our pot.
We pour it in our bowls, and we eat it all up!

# Fingerplays and Songs

### 179 Chopstick Song (to the tune of "Dreidel")

Pass out straws or chopsticks to use with this song, or have children mime eating with chopsticks throughout.

I have two little chopsticks,
I got them at the store.
I use them to eat my rice
And then I eat some more!

Oh, chopsticks, chopsticks, chopsticks,
I use them every day.
Chopsticks, chopsticks, chopsticks,
I use them just this way.

I'm eating with my chopsticks,
I'm eating rice at last.
But now I am so hungry
That I eat with them real fast!

Sing/mime quickly.

Oh, chopsticks, chopsticks, chopsticks,
I use them every day.
Chopsticks, chopsticks, chopsticks,
I use them just this way.

I'm eating with my chopsticks,
There's rice left, don't you know?
But now I'm getting full
So I'm eating very slow.

Sing/mime slowly.

Oh, chopsticks, chopsticks, chopsticks,
I use them every day.
Chopsticks, chopsticks, chopsticks,
I use them just this way.

## 180 *El Chocolate*: A Traditional Latin American Folk Song

Teach the following Spanish vocabulary, and then share the rhyme below. Invite the children to count on their fingers and mime stirring a cup of cocoa.

> one: *uno* (OO-no)
> two: *dos* (DOSE)
> three: *tres* (TRACE)
> stir: *bate* (BAH-teh)
> chocolate: *chocolate* (CHO-ko-LAH-teh)

*Uno, dos, tres, CHO*
*Uno, dos, tres, CO*
*Uno, dos, tres, LA*
*Uno, dos, tres, TE*
*Chocolate, chocolate,*
*Bate, bate chocolate!*
*Chocolate, chocolate,*
*Bate, bate chocolate!*

## 181 *Un Huevito* (un oo-ay-VEE-to) / Little Egg: A Nursery Rhyme from Spain

This little finger bought a little egg, (*touch pinky*)
This little finger cooked it, (*touch ring finger*)
This little finger sprinkled salt on top, (*touch middle finger*)
This little finger tasted it, (*touch index finger*)
And this naughty thumb gobbled it all up! (*touch thumb*)

### 182 Crepe Song

Crepes are delicious thin pancakes from France. This action rhyme is based on "Pancake Song" by poet Christina Rossetti (1830–1894). Invite the children to act out the actions as you say the rhyme.

Mix the batter.
Stir it up.
Pour it in the pan.
Cook the crepe.
Toss the crepe.
Catch it if you can!

# Craft

### 183 Magic Pasta Pot

Based on *Strega Nona* by Tomie dePaola (New York: Simon and Schuster, 1975). In this classic retelling of an old Italian folktale, dim-witted Big Anthony gets more than he bargains for when he tries to use Strega Nona's magic pasta pot.

*Materials:* paper cups, craft sticks, white yarn, red processing stickers or circles cut from red construction paper, glue

*Preparation:*

1. Cut twenty 12-inch lengths of white yarn for each child.
2. Hold the twenty strands together and tie a knot in the middle.
3. Punch a small hole in the bottom of each paper cup.

*Directions:*

1. Spread glue on one end of the craft stick.
2. Push the glue-covered end of the craft stick into the middle of the knot in the yarn clump.
3. Decorate the strands with red processing dots to represent meatballs.
4. Push the stick into the cup and down through the hole in the bottom.
5. When Big Anthony says the magic words, push the stick up so that the pasta pot makes more spaghetti!

# 20

# Forest Animals

· · · · · · · · · · · · · · · · · · · · · · · · · · · · · · · · · · ·

## Books

**184  *Mole's Hill* by Lois Ehlert. New York: Harcourt, 1994.**

Set in the woodlands of Wisconsin, this story is based on a Seneca tale. When Fox decides that Mole's hill is in the way of his path and must go, Mole comes up with a clever way to show how important her hill is. Ehlert's bright illustrations incorporate the appliqué and sewn beadwork forms of the Woodland Indians.

**185  *A Home for Pearl Squirrel* by Amy Crane Johnson. Green Bay, WI: Raven Tree, 2004.**

This bilingual Spanish/English text features Pearl the squirrel, who is excited to show off her new home to the other forest animals. But she soon discovers that a squirrel's home is not the best home for all the animals, even though it's the best home for her. After reading the story, discuss why various animals, such as squirrels, mice, birds, and rabbits, make their homes in certain places.

**186  \*Rabbit's Gift* by George Shannon. New York: Harcourt, 2007.**

This is a retelling of the fable that originated in China. When Rabbit finds two turnips, he decides to share them with his friends in the forest. Soon everyone is sharing their food and generosity.

**187  *Thanks to the Animals* by Allen Sockabasin. Gardiner, ME: Tilbury House, 2005.**

During the 1900 Passamaquoddy winter migration in Maine, baby Zoo Sap falls off the family bobsled and is protected by the forest animals until his father comes back for him. Audio files of the author reading the story in Passamaquoddy, the language of the Native American tribes who once occupied the land between Maine and New Brunswick, Canada, are available on the publisher's website at www.tilburyhouse.com.

# Flannelboards

### 188 Why Opossum Has a Bare Tail: A Creek Indian Tale

One day, Opossum was walking in the woods around sunset when he spied Raccoon. Now Opossum had always admired Raccoon because he had a beautiful tail with rings all around it.

So Opossum went up to Raccoon and said, "How did you get those pretty rings on your tail?"

Raccoon stroked his fluffy long tail fondly. "Well, I wrapped bark around the tail here and here and here," he said, pointing. "Then I stuck my tail into the fire. The fur between the strips of bark turned black and the places underneath the bark remained brown, just as you see!"

Opossum thanked Raccoon and hurried away to gather some bark. He wrapped the bark around his furry tail, built a big bonfire, and stuck his tail into the flames. Only the bonfire was too hot and too fierce. It instantly burned all the hair off Opossum's tail, leaving it entirely bare.

Opossum wailed and moaned when he saw his poor tail, but there was nothing he could do but wait for the fur to grow back. Opossum waited and waited and waited. But the tail was too badly burnt by the fire, and the fur did not grow back. Opossum's tail remained bare for the rest of his life.

Opossum tails have been bare ever since.

### 189 *Grandfather Tang's Story: A Tale Told with Tangrams* by Ann Tompert. New York: Crown, 1990.

This story of two magical, shape-changing foxes uses tangrams, traditional Chinese puzzles. A tangram begins with a square, which is then cut into seven standard pieces. As the story is told, the pieces are rearranged to make different shapes. Follow the directions in the back of the book to create your own tangram out of felt or magnet-backed paper, and then tell the story of the foxes using your flannelboard or magnetboard. Diagrams for each animal shape can be found in the book.

# Fingerplays and Songs

### 190 *The Turkey: A Traditional Rhyme from Hungary

This old road is hard and bumpy, (*mime driving on a bumpy road*)
Our new turkey's wild and jumpy. (*jump*)
Driver! Driver! Not so jerky! (*shake finger*)
You will make us lose our turkey. (*mime grabbing at escaping turkey*)

### 191 *Firefly, Firefly: A Traditional Rhyme from Italy

Firefly, firefly, yellow and bright,
Bridle the horse under your light.
The son of the king is ready to ride,
Firefly, firefly, fly by my side.

**192  \*In the Forest: A Song in ASL and English** (to the tune of "The Wheels on the Bus")

The RABBITS in the forest go hop, hop, hop,
Hop, hop, hop, hop, hop, hop.
The RABBITS in the forest go hop, hop, hop,
All day long.

The BIRDS in the forest go flap, flap, flap . . .
The SQUIRRELS in the forest go climb, climb, climb . . .
The DEER in the forest go run, run, run . . .
The FROGS in the forest go ribbit, ribbit, ribbit . . .
The BEARS in the forest go grr, grr, grr . . .

# Craft

**193  ASL Deer Mask**

This fun mask shows the ASL sign DEER.

*Materials:* deer face and ears cut from light-brown construction paper (from template on website), large muzzle piece cut from black construction paper (from template on website), small muzzle piece cut from white construction paper (from template on website), two hands cut from brown or black construction paper (from template on website), black processing dots, googly eyes, craft stick, glue, crayons

*Directions:*

1. Glue the small muzzle piece at the bottom of the large muzzle piece.
2. Glue the large muzzle piece at the bottom of the face.
3. Glue the ears to the sides of the head.
4. Glue the hands to either side of the head, slightly above the ears with the thumbs touching the top of the head. These are the antlers and also show the sign DEER.

5. Glue googly eyes onto the face.
6. Stick a black processing dot onto the top of the small white muzzle piece for the nose.
7. Glue a craft stick to the back of the face so that it can be used as a mask.

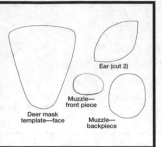

# 21
# Friends

• • • • • • • • • • • • • • • • • • • • • • • • • • • • • • • • • •

## Books

**194  *Caribbean Dream* by Rachel Isadora. New York: Putnam, 1998.**

Simple text and colorful illustrations follow a group of children through a day in their Caribbean home. After reading the story, ask the children how the activities in the story are the same as and different from the things they do with their own friends.

**195  *Lissy's Friends* by Grace Lin. New York: Viking, 2007.**

Lissy, an Asian American girl, is the new girl at school and has a hard time making friends—so she makes a variety of origami animals to be her friends. When she takes them to the playground, the wind blows them all away. But Lissy makes a real friend with a girl who wants to learn how to make a crane herself. Follow up the story by making a paper crane using the directions in the back of the book.

**196  *All Kinds of Friends, Even Green* by Ellen B. Senisi. Bethesda, MD: Woodbine House, 2002.**

Moses considers all the different kinds of friends he has as he ponders which to write about for a school assignment. This winsome story incorporates information about disabilities—Moses has spina bifida and uses a wheelchair—without becoming preachy or heavy-handed.

**197  *The Garden Wall* by Phyllis Limbacher Tildes. Watertown, MA: Charlesbridge, 2006.**

Tim is taken aback when he learns that his new neighbor is not only a girl but also deaf. When he is assigned to work with her to perform a fable at school, he's nervous—but as he gets to know Maria, their performance of "The Hearing Country Mouse and the Deaf City Mouse" comes together, and they become friends. This story introduces some basic American Sign Language as well as information about the technology used by people who are deaf.

# Flannelboard

### 198  Four Friends: A Folktale from Bhutan

This story also lends itself to a prop story presentation. Use puppets or stuffed animals for the animal characters, and create an apple tree by gluing red pom-poms onto a long-handled dish sponge.

Once upon a time, Peacock planted an apple seed. "I am going to grow an apple tree!" she said.
  Up hopped Rabbit. "You are going to grow an apple tree? Oooo, can I help?"
  "Yes," said Peacock. "You can water the seed."
  So Rabbit watered the seed.
  Monkey saw her. "Oooo, you are watering the seed. Can I help?"
  "Yes," said Rabbit. "You can feed the seed."
  So Monkey found some nice rich fertilizer and fed the seed.
  Elephant saw him. "Oooo, you are feeding the seed. Can I help?"
  "Yes," said Monkey. "You can watch the seed."
  So Elephant watched the seed to make sure that no birds or other creatures ate it. Elephant watched for a long, long time. And do you know what happened? That seed grew into an apple tree!
  Along came Peacock, Rabbit, and Monkey. They were all so pleased with what their cooperation had done. "Elephant," said the others, "you have spent so many hours watching the seed, you ought to have the first apple."
  Elephant reached up into the branches, but . . .
  "I can't reach the apples!" he cried.
  "I can help!" called Monkey. He climbed up onto Elephant's back and reached up into the branches, but . . .
  "I can't reach the apples!" he cried.
  "I can help!" called Rabbit. She climbed up onto Monkey's back and reached up into the branches, but . . .
  "I can't reach the apples!" she cried.
  "I can help!" called Peacock. She climbed up onto Rabbit's back and reached up into the branches, and pulled down many sweet apples, enough for all four friends to share.
  The four friends sat in the shade of their tree, enjoying the sweet, juicy apples.

# Fingerplays and Songs

### 199  Friends Around the World

Let's take a trip around the world,
And say hello to all the boys and girls.

Our first stop is a country shaped like a boot,
Say, "*Ciao, amici!*" (chow a-MEE-chee) in Italy and give a hoot.

If you happen to get a chance,
Say, "*Bonjour, amis!*" (bone-ZHOOR ah-mee) when in France.

In the morning when greeting friends,
The Japanese say, "*Konnichiwa, tomodachi!*" (ko-NEE-chee-wa toe-mo-DAH-chee) to them.

"*Hola, amigos!*" (OH-la ah-MEE-goes) is how we say hello,
To our friends in Mexico.

Sweden is a land of snow and ice,
Saying "*Goddag, kamrat*" (go-DAG kam-RAT) is awfully nice.

There are many lands to travel to and see,
Saying hello and making friends is as easy as 1, 2, 3!

### 200  Hello

As I was walking down the street, down the street, down the street,
My little friend I chanced to meet, and so I said, "Hello."

But in China walking down the street, down the street, down the street,
In China, walking down the street, people say, "*Ni hao!*" (nee-how)

But in Africa walking down the street, down the street, down the street,
In Africa, walking down the street, people say, "*Jambo!*" (JAM-bo)

But in Israel walking down the street, down the street, down the street,
In Israel, walking down the street, people say, "*Shalom!*" (sha-LOHM)

### 201  "Circle of Friends" from *Multicultural Bean Bag Fun* by Georgiana Stewart. Long Branch, NJ: Kimbo Educational, 2009.

This song features different activities to do with your beanbag as it mentions kids from many lands.

### 202  "*Mi Jachol Lassim* (Israel)" from *Children's Folk Dances* by Georgiana Stewart. Long Branch, NJ: Kimbo Educational, 1998.

This movement song combines an Israeli folk melody with English words about friends that encourage kids to clap, pat, tap, and dance.

# Craft

### 203 ASL Friends Magnet

This craft shows the ASL sign for FRIEND.

*Materials:* two hands die-cut or precut from construction paper, glue, crayons or markers, adhesive magnets

*Directions:*

1. On each hand, fold and glue down the pinky, ring finger, middle finger, and thumb.
2. Lay one hand facing up. Turn the other hand over and lay it so that the index finger forms a diagonal with the index finger of the first hand.
3. Fold the ends of each index finger over so that the two fingers "lock" together. Glue them together where the two fingers touch at front and back.
4. Decorate the hands as desired.
5. Stick two magnetic strips on the back of the hands.

# 22
# Frogs

• • • • • • • • • • • • • • • • • • • • • • • • • • • • • • • • • • • •

## Books

**204** ***The Wide-Mouthed Frog* by Keith Faulkner. New York: Dial, 1996.**

This pop-up version of a beloved tale from the American South features a frog who boasts about his wide mouth . . . until he meets an alligator who eats wide-mouthed frogs!

**205** ***Screen of Frogs: An Old Tale* by Sheila Hamanaka. New York: Orchard, 1993.**

Koji, the spoiled son of wealthy landowners in old Japan, learns respect for nature and for hard work after an encounter with a magical frog creature.

**206** ***Jump, Frog, Jump!* by Robert Kalan. New York: Greenwillow, 1995.**

In this cumulative tale, a frog tries to catch a fly without getting caught himself. After reading this book, teach the children the refrain "jump, frog, jump," in Spanish: "*salto de la rana, salta*" (SAHL-toe day la RAH-nah SAHL-ta). Then reread the book having the children say the refrain in Spanish.

**207** ***The Biggest Frog in Australia* by Susan L. Roth. New York: Simon and Schuster, 1996.**

When a thirsty frog drinks up all the water in Australia, the other animals try to make him give it up. Based on an Australian folktale, this book introduces Australian vocabulary and wildlife.

# Flannelboards

## 208  The Frog Maiden: A Folktale from Burma (Myanmar)

Adapted from a story in *Burmese Folk-Tales* by Maung Htin Aung (Calcutta: Geoffrey Cumberlege, Oxford University Press, 1948).

Once upon a time, in a country called Burma, there lived a man and woman who were expecting a baby. But when the baby was born, they got a big surprise. It wasn't a human baby at all, but a little frog! The little frog spoke and acted like a human child, and her parents and all in the neighborhood grew to love her.

The frog maiden grew up. When she was a young lady frog, her mother died, and her father remarried. But his new wife had two grown daughters who were ugly and jealous of Little Miss Frog's popularity.

One day the king's youngest son announced that he would go to the royal pool and perform the hair-washing ceremony. He invited all young ladies to come, because after he washed his hair he would pick one of them to marry.

The ugly stepsisters were so excited. They dressed in their best clothes and started down the road for the ceremony. The frog maiden ran after them, pleading to join them.

The stepsisters laughed. "The prince has invited all the young ladies, not young frogs!"

Nevertheless, the frog maiden followed them to the ceremony, where there were hundreds of young ladies gathered around a pool full of lilies.

The prince came and washed his hair in the pool. The young ladies did the same. At the end of the ceremony, the prince said, "Young ladies, you are all so beautiful I don't know which of you to pick! I will throw a bouquet of jasmines into the air, and whichever lady it lands on shall be my princess."

So he threw the bouquet into the air, and it landed on the frog maiden! The prince was disappointed, but he felt he ought to keep his word. So the frog maiden married the prince, and became Princess Frog.

Not long after that, the king called the prince and his brothers to him and said, "I am growing too old to rule, and I need to choose an heir. I love you all so much that it is difficult to decide, so I shall set a task for you to perform, and whichever of you does it best shall become king. Here is your task: bring me a golden deer in seven days."

The youngest prince went home to Princess Frog and told her about the task.

"What, only a golden deer!" exclaimed Princess Frog. "Do not worry, darling. I will give you the golden deer."

So the youngest prince stayed at home, trusting his wife, while his brothers went into the forest in search of the deer.

On the seventh day, Princess Frog woke her husband and said, "Here is your golden deer."

The young prince looked and there in his bedroom was a deer made of pure gold! He took it to the palace, and to the great annoyance of the elder princes who brought ordinary deer, he was declared the heir.

The other princes begged for a second chance, so the king said, "Very well, I will give you a second task. In seven days, bring me rice that never becomes stale, and meat that never goes bad."

The youngest prince went home and told Princess Frog about the new task.

"Don't worry, sweet prince," said Princess Frog. "I will give you the rice and meat."

So the youngest prince stayed at home, trusting his wife, while his brothers went in search of the rice and meat.

On the seventh day, Princess Frog woke her husband and said, "Here is your rice and meat."

The youngest prince took the rice and meat and went to the palace, and to the great annoyance of the other princes who brought only well-cooked rice and meat, he was again declared the heir.

But the other princes begged for one more chance, so the king said, "This is absolutely the last task. In seven days, bring me the most beautiful woman on this earth."

The other princes laughed, for they had very beautiful wives, and they knew that their brother had only Princess Frog. "Surely we will win this time!" they said.

When the prince reached home, he said sadly to his wife, "I must go and seek out the most beautiful woman on earth."

"Don't worry, sweet prince," replied Princess Frog. "Take me to the palace. Surely I shall be declared the most beautiful woman."

The prince didn't want to hurt her feelings, so he agreed. But he knew that he would not win the contest this time.

On the seventh day, Princess Frog woke her husband and said, "It is time to go to the palace."

The prince opened his eyes, hoping that, somehow, his wife had been able to make herself beautiful. But she was still a frog and as ugly as ever.

Still, he didn't want to hurt her feelings, so he took her to the palace. The other princes were already there with their beautiful wives.

The king said, "Where is your beautiful woman?"

And the frog princess said, "I am his beautiful woman."

With that, she took off her frog skin. There stood a beautiful woman in silk and satin. The king declared her the most beautiful woman in the world and selected the prince to be his heir.

After that, Princess Frog stayed in her beautiful woman form . . . except when she wanted to go for a swim. That was more fun to do in her frog skin.

And they all lived happily ever after.

### 209  How Frog Got Eyes and Mole Got a Tail: An African American Pourquoi Tale

Adapted from "Why Frog Got Eyes and Mole Got Tail" in *What's the Hurry, Fox? and Other Animal Stories* by Joyce Carol Oates (New York: HarperCollins, 2004).

In the beginning, Frog had a long tail, but no eyes. He would sit all day and listen to the water splashing around him and the flies buzzing, but he couldn't see them.

In the beginning, Mole had great big eyes, but he didn't have a tail. Every day he would dig deep into the earth, and his eyes would get full of dirt. When he finished digging, he would have to spend a long time wiping the dirt out of his eyes.

One day, Mole happened to dig his way out of a hole near where Frog was sitting on his lily pad, listening to the water and the flies.

Mole said, "Hey, Brer Frog, what do you want with that big old tail anyway? It's not doing you any good."

And Frog said, "You're right, Brer Mole. Say, what do you want with those big old eyes? They don't do you any good digging underground in the dark."

Mole said, "Let's swap!"

So they did. And ever since, Frog has had big eyes and no tail, and Mole has had a long tail and no eyes.

Frog without eyes

# Fingerplays and Songs

### 210 *Froggy Frolic: A Song in ASL and English

Cut the end off an old tube sock and place it over your arm to be the log. Make frogs out of pom-poms with googly eyes and use Velcro to attach them to the sock. To make the frogs sit on the log, do the sign SIT on your forearm instead of on your palm. Then show the frogs jumping into the water by moving the sign forward off the log.

FIVE green and speckled FROGS SAT on a speckled log
EATING some most delicious bugs. (Yum yum!)
ONE jumped into a pool, where it was nice and COOL.
Now there are FOUR green and speckled FROGS.

FOUR green and speckled FROGS . . .
THREE green and speckled FROGS . . .
TWO green and speckled FROGS . . .

ONE green and speckled FROG sat on a speckled log
EATING some most delicious bugs. (Yum yum!)
He jumped into a pool where it was nice and COOL.
Now there are no (NONE) green and speckled FROGS.

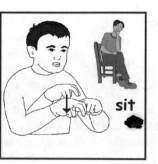

**211** *"Sma Grodorna (Sweden)"* from *Children's Folk Dances* by Georgiana Stewart. Long Branch, NJ: Kimbo Educational, 1998.

This musical movement riddle combines a Swedish folk melody with an engaging jumping game.

**212** *"El Coqui"* from *De Colores and Other Latin American Folk Songs for Children* by Jose-Luis Orozco. Berkeley, CA: Arcoiris Records, 1996.

This song, entirely in Spanish, is a traditional folk song about a little frog that lives in Puerto Rico. Before playing the song, explain that *coqui* (ko-KEE) is the Spanish word for a particular kind of frog and that "*coqui*" is also the sound that this frog makes. Have the children crouch down like frogs. Tell them to listen carefully to the song. Each time they hear the word *coqui*, they should jump like a frog!

# Craft

### 213 Poison Dart Frog Puppet

Poison dart frogs are small poisonous frogs from the rain forests of South and Central America. Some South American Indians use the poison on the tips of their hunting arrows and blowgun darts. Poison dart frogs come in bright colors such as red, blue, and yellow with black markings on them. Their colors serve as a warning to predators that the frogs are poisonous!

*Materials:* red, yellow, and blue construction paper, rectangular strip of red construction paper for the tongue, googly eyes, glue, crayons

*Directions:*

1. Fold a piece of construction paper in thirds, forming a long rectangle.
2. Fold the rectangle in fourths, making a W shape.
3. Draw or glue eyes on the right outside part of the W.
4. Glue the tongue to the inside center of the W.
5. Decorate the frog as desired with crayons.
6. Your fingers and thumb will fit in the open top parts of the W so that you can open the frog puppet's mouth!

# 23
# Gardens and Growing

## Books

**214** ***The Empty Pot* by Demi. New York: Henry Holt, 1990.**

In this Chinese folktale, Ping is a boy who has a truly green thumb—but when the emperor passes out seeds for all the children to grow, nothing Ping does will make his sprout. Downhearted, he appears before the emperor, the only child with an empty pot, knowing he has done his best—and is rewarded for his honesty. All the seeds had been cooked, and Ping was the only child willing to admit that his seed did not grow. After reading, ask the children why they think the emperor gave out cooked seeds.

**215** ***Jamie O'Rourke and the Big Potato: An Irish Folktale* by Tomie dePaola. New York: Putnam, 1992.**

When a leprechaun tricks Jamie O'Rourke into wishing for a giant potato instead of gold, the whole village has to help Jamie move it.

**216** ***The Ugly Vegetables* by Grace Lin. Watertown, MA: Charlesbridge, 1999.**

A little girl thinks her mom's garden is the ugliest in the world until she discovers how delicious the Chinese vegetables growing there really are. If possible, get some of the vegetables listed in the back of the book from an Asian market to show the children. Ask the children to compare these vegetables to more familiar ones such as carrots and potatoes. How are they the same and different?

**217** ***One Leaf Rides the Wind: Counting in a Japanese Garden* by Celeste Davidson Mannis. New York: Viking, 2002.**

A series of descriptive haiku count through the delights of a Japanese garden. After reading the story, introduce the rules of the haiku form and work with the children to write their own haiku about a garden.

# Flannelboards

### 218 *Andiamo, Weasel!* by Rose Marie Grant. New York: Knopf, 2002.

Set in Italy and sprinkled with Italian vocabulary, this satisfying tale centers around an industrious crow and the sneaky weasel who tries to trick her into doing all the work.

### 219 *The Gigantic Turnip* by Aleksei Tolstoy. Cambridge, MA: Barefoot Books, 1998.

In this funny retelling of a Russian folktale, an old woman and old man need lots of help to pick a turnip that won't stop growing.

# Fingerplays and Songs

### 220 *Cinco Verde Guisantes* / **Five Green Peas** (adapted traditional)

*Cinco verde guisantes* (SINK-oh VAIR-deh gee-SAHN-tays) in a pea pod pressed, *(make fist)*
*Uno* (OO-no),
*Dos* (DOSE),
*Tres* (TRACE),
*Cuatro* (KWA-troe),
*Cinco* (SINK-oh). *(lift fingers one at a time)*
They grew and grew and did not stop *(stretch fingers out)*
Till one day that pea pod popped! *(clap hands)*

### 221 *Five Little Flowers: A Rhyme in ASL and English

FIVE little FLOWERS grew outside my door.
I gave ONE to my MOTHER, and then there were FOUR.
FOUR little FLOWERS, so pretty to see.
I gave ONE to my FATHER, and then there were THREE.
THREE little FLOWERS, and I knew what to do.

I gave ONE to my BROTHER, and then there were TWO.
TWO little FLOWERS, growing in the sun.
I gave ONE to my SISTER, and then there was ONE.
ONE little FLOWER, I thought it would be fun
To give that ONE to YOU, and then there were NONE.

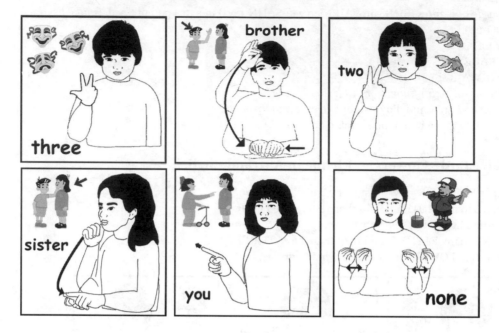

**222** **"Planting Rice" from *Multicultural Bean Bag Fun* by Georgiana Stewart. Long Branch, NJ: Kimbo Educational, 2009.**

Based on a Philippine rice planting song, this action song encourages kids to use their beanbags as they pretend to plant rice.

# Craft

**223** **Paper *Mola* Garden**

*Molas* are the brightly colored appliqué panels made in the San Blas region of Panama by the Kuna Indians. The Kunas have resided in the Panama/Colombia area for centuries.

*Materials:* a piece of black construction paper, brightly colored flower and vegetable shapes cut in three sizes (small, medium, large), strips of green construction paper, strips of brown construction paper, glue

*Directions:*

1. Choose an item to begin with such as a flower. Select it in three colors and sizes.
2. Glue the largest item to the black construction paper. Leaving a thin border, glue the second color on top of the first item. Repeat with the third and smallest item.
3. Repeat with other designs and items until you have created the garden picture of your choice.

# 24
# Hair

. . . . . . . . . . . . . . . . . . . . . . . . . . . . . . . . . . . . .

## Books

**224** ***Minji's Salon*** **by Eun-hee Choung. La Jolla, CA: Kane/Miller, 2008.**

As her mother visits the local salon, Minji, a young South Korean girl, sets up a salon of her own at home, with the dog as her client. Children will giggle at the juxtaposition of the calm, professional salon pictured on the left-hand side of each spread with Minji's improvised salon on the right.

**225** ***ASL Tales: Rapunzel*** **by Judy Hood. Created and performed in American Sign Language by Pinky Aiello. Calgary, AB: ASL Tales, 2008.**

This book and DVD package presents an updated version of the classic German fairy tale. The DVD presents the illustrations along with the story told in English and American Sign Language. Children will love seeing Pinky Aiello, one of the top ASL storytellers in the world, present her signed version of the story along with the English narration. After viewing the story, show children the vocabulary section on the DVD to help them learn some of the signs used in the story.

**226** ***Happy to Be Nappy*** **by bell hooks. New York: Hyperion, 1999.**

A rhyming celebration of African American girls' hair. Follow up with a comparison of textures. Ask the children to think of ways to describe how hair feels.

**227** ***Erandi's Braids*** **by Antonio Hernandez Madrigal. New York: Putnam, 1999.**

Erandi lives in a small Mexican village, and her long, beautiful black braids are her greatest source of pride. But when a barber comes from the city offering lots of money for her hair, she sells it in order to buy her mother a new fishing net.

# Flannelboard

**228** *****"Yasha" from *Babushka's Mother Goose* by Patricia Polacco. New York: Penguin, 1995.**

Using the flannelboard patterns, make Yasha's face, the fence, the barn, the dog, the goat, the hill, and the hare. Cut a slit in Yasha's face where indicated on the pattern, then cut a length of fake fur so that it will fit the slit. Place the other objects on the flannelboard and position Yasha's face over the board. Then, as you recite the poem, feed the fake-fur beard through the slit so that it covers the objects below.

# Fingerplays and Songs

**229 All Who Want to Sail: A Rhyme from Belgium**

All who want to sail, (*cup hands to make boat*)
Must have beards. (*move cupped hands down from chin to represent beard*)
John, Pete, Joris, Cornell,
They have beards, they have beards.
John, Pete, Joris, and Cornell,
They have beards, so come on board! (*spread arms wide*)

Repeat, using the names of the children in your group.

**230 Rapunzel**

Inspired by the German fairy tale.

Rapunzel, Rapunzel was locked in a tower,
Where she couldn't see the sun or even a flower. (*look up and down*)
By day and by night she longed to be free,
But as for how, she just couldn't see. (*lift shoulders in a shrug*)

Then one day a handsome prince
Rode by on his horse and blew her a kiss. (*blow kiss*)
Rapunzel, Rapunzel, let down your golden hair,
I will help you escape from up there. (*point up*)

Rapunzel's hair fell down to the ground,
And the prince rescued her without a sound. (*fingers to lips, "shhh"*)
Away they rode on his fine horse,
And lived happily ever after, of course! (*pretend to gallop away*)

### 231 Michael Finnigan: A Traditional Song from Ireland

There was a boy called Michael Finnigan,
He grew whiskers on his chin-igan. (*draw hands down from chin*)
The wind came out and blew them in again. (*raise hands back up to chin*)
Poor old Michael Finnigan, begin again.

Repeat, growing faster each time.

### 232 Hair (to the tune of "London Bridge")

I have long hair tumbling down, tumbling down, tumbling down.
I have long hair tumbling down, and I like it just that way!

My hair is short and blond, short and blond, short and blond.
My hair is short and blond, and I like it just that way!

I have brown wavy hair, brown wavy hair, brown wavy hair.
I have brown wavy hair, and I like it just that way!

My hair is kinky and black, kinky and black, kinky and black.
My hair is kinky and black, and I like it just that way!

All hair is beautiful, beautiful, beautiful.
All hair is beautiful, and we love it all!

# Craft

### 233 Ukrainian Headdress Festival Wreath

A wreath headdress is made from leaves, flowers, and branches. It is typically worn on festive occasions and on holy days. In Ukraine, a headdress is worn by girls and young unmarried women, and it remains part of the Ukrainian national costume.

*Materials:* paper plate with the middle cut out, flowers and leaves cut from construction paper, two 18-inch pieces of ribbon, crayons, glue

*Directions:*

1. Color the paper plate ring.
2. Glue flower and leaf shapes onto the ring.
3. Tie the pieces of ribbon to the back of the ring and leave the ends to hang loose.

# 25
# Hands

• • • • • • • • • • • • • • • • • • • • • • • • • • • • •

## Books

**234** *To Be an Artist* **by Maya Ajmera and John D. Ivanko. Watertown, MA: Charlesbridge, 2004.**

With gorgeous full-color illustrations of children around the world, this book celebrates the many ways of making art. For storytime, read only the large text on each page. If desired, share some of the information in the small print as the children look at the pictures.

**235** *Nadia's Hands* **by Karen English. Honesdale, PA: Boyds Mills Press, 1999.**

Nadia, a Pakistani American girl, is nervous about the *mehndi* (traditional henna painted designs) that will remain on her hands after she acts as flower girl in her aunt's wedding, but when she realizes how important the tradition is to her family, she learns to value it as well.

**236** *\*Tools* **by Ann Morris. New York: Lothrop, Lee and Shepard, 1992.**

One of the things we do with our hands is making and using tools. In this book, simple text and color photos explore different types of tools around the world. The text emphasizes the common uses of tools, while the photos show the variety of types of tools and their use in different cultures. A photo index identifies the origins of all the tools discussed.

**237** *The Handmade Alphabet* **by Laura Rankin. New York: Dial, 1991.**

Letter by letter, this beautifully illustrated book demonstrates the ASL manual alphabet. On each page, a hand shows the letter, while an object or a concept beginning with that letter is shown in the picture (for example, the hand showing *e* is being erased). Invite the children to identify the object or concept that goes with the letter, then to sign each letter with you. Reinforce the manual alphabet by signing random letters and asking the children to come up with words that start with the letter.

## Flannelboard

**238 Matching Mittens: A Song in Spanish and English** (to the tune of "The Wheels on the Bus")

We wear mittens when it's cold outside, cold outside, cold outside,
We wear mittens when it's cold outside, to keep our hands warm.
If you have a mitten of *azul* (ah-SOOL), of *azul*, of *azul*,
If you have a mitten of *azul*, bring it up here now.

. . . *rojo* (ROH-ho) . . .
. . . *verde* (VAIR-deh) . . .
. . . *blanco* (BLAHN-co) . . .
. . . *rosa* (ROH-sah) . . .
. . . *amarillo* (ah-mah-REE-yo) . . .

## Fingerplays and Songs

**239 Hello Hands**

All around the world
People use their hands to say hello.
I bet you know to wave and say "Hi!"
But there are others, did you know?

In India, you press your palms together
And say, "*Namaste*." (NA-ma-stay)
In Hawaii, put up thumb and pinky
And say "Aloha!" today. (ah-LOE-ha)

In Thailand, put your palms together
And give a little bow.
Say "*Sawatdee!*" (SAH-WAT-dee)
And you will be greeting someone now.

About the gestures:

In India and many parts of Asia, the gesture of palms pressed together shows respect and greeting.

In Hawaii, the *shaka* sign (thumb and pinky raised with the palm facing you) is a gesture of friendship and greeting.

In Thailand, the *wai,* or the gesture of hands pressed together while bowing, is a common way to greet someone, show thanks, or apologize. The higher the hands are held and the lower the bow, the more respect is being shown.

**240** **\*Close Hands, Open Hands: A Traditional Japanese Rhyme**

Close hands, open hands,
Clap hands, close hands.
Open hands, clap hands,
Raise hands up.
Close hands, open hands,
Clap hands, close hands.

**241** **"Mexican Handclapping Song" from *Multicultural Children's Songs* by Ella Jenkins. Washington, DC: Smithsonian Folkways, 1995.**

This simple song with Mexican roots encourages listening and using basic Spanish vocabulary, as well as clapping and silly dancing.

**242** **Signing, Signing** (to the tune of "A Bicycle Built for Two")

Show the signs in parentheses as you sing the song.

SIGNING, SIGNING,
It's what we LIKE to do.
We know SIGN LANGUAGE is a way to talk too.
You DON'T KNOW what you're missin'
'Til you use your EYES to listen.
Talk with your hands,
We'll UNDERSTAND,
'Cause we love SIGN LANGUAGE too!

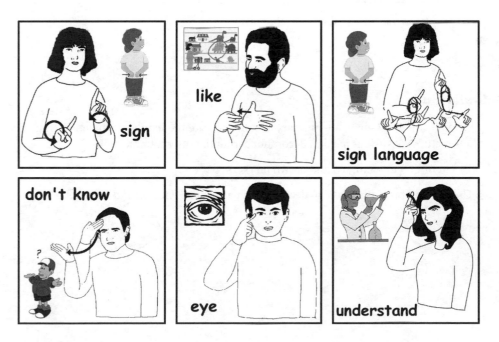

**243 Hands** (to the tune of "Three Blind Mice")

Hands, hands, hands.
Hands, hands, hands.
Clap your hands.
Clap your hands.
Now shake hands with your neighbor there,
Next wave your hands high in the air,
And wiggle your fingers as fast as you dare.
Hands, hands, hands.
Here's how you say "hands" in Spanish: *manos!* (MAH-nohs)

Repeat song, replacing "hands" with *manos.* If desired, repeat using "hands" in other languages:

Chinese: *shǒu* (shaw)
French: *les mains* (lay MEH)
Dutch: *handen* (HAHN-den)
American Sign Language:

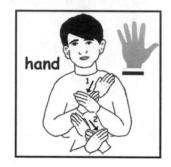

# Craft

**244 Mehndi Hands**

*Mehndi* is the application of henna, a temporary dye, to decorate the hands of women in India and Pakistan. Show pictures of various *mehndi* decorations from the Internet or a book.

*Materials:* die-cut or precut hand, red and brown markers

*Directions:* Use red and brown markers to decorate the paper hand with *mehndi* designs.

# 26
# Hats

. . . . . . . . . . . . . . . . . . . . . . . . . . . . . . . . . . . .

## Books

**245** *The Hatseller and the Monkeys* by Baba Wagué Diakité. New York: Scholastic, 1999.

Though many kids might be familiar with *Caps for Sale* by Esphyr Slobodkina, most don't realize the story is based on a West African folktale. Diakité brings the original story to life, with attention to cultural details and traditional styles of artwork.

**246** *Aunt Flossie's Hats (and Crab Cakes Later)* by Elizabeth Fitzgerald Howard. New York: Clarion, 1991.

Two African American girls visit their elderly Aunt Flossie, who tells them about her past through her hat collection.

**247** *\*Hats Hats Hats* by Ann Morris. New York: Mulberry, 1989.

Simple text and colorful photos explore hats around the world. The text examines all the things hats have in common, and a pictorial index identifies the location of each hat pictured. After reading the story, go through the pictures again and ask the children to identify ways the hats pictured are similar to and different from their own.

**248** *What's the Matter, Habibi?* by Betsy Lewin. New York: Clarion, 1997.

Habibi the camel spends his days following Ahmed in a circle as he gives rides to children in an Egyptian bazaar. But one day Habibi takes a trip through the bazaar in search of what he pines for—his very own fez.

## Flannelboard

**249** ***Uncle Nacho's Hat: A Folktale from Nicaragua*** **by Harriet Rohmer. San Francisco: Children's Book Press, 1989.**

When Uncle Nacho's niece gives him a new hat, he tries to dispose of the old one, but it keeps coming back to him.

## Fingerplays and Songs

**250  *My Hat Has Three Corners: A Rhyme from Brazil** (adapted traditional)

Before saying this rhyme, hold up a cutout of a triangle. Have the children count the sides with you. Then invite the children to step in the shape of a triangle on the floor with each line of the rhyme.

My hat has three corners,
Three corners has my hat.
If it didn't have three corners,
It wouldn't be my hat.

Now hold up a square and say "Is this my hat? Let's count the sides." Then repeat the stepping rhyme. Continue with a rectangle, pentagon, hexagon, octagon, and circle. This activity reinforces shape awareness and gross motor skills.

**251  *Bat, Bat, Come Under My Hat: A Traditional Rhyme from England**

Bat, bat, come under my hat,
And I'll give you a slice of bacon.
And when I bake,
I'll give you a cake,
If I am not mistaken.

**252** **"Mexican Hat Dance"** from *Put On Your Dancing Shoes* by Joanie Bartels. Los Angeles: Purple Frog Records, 2001.

Place hats around the floor and have the children dance around them with maracas and other instruments.

# Craft

**253** **Chinese Paper Bowl Hat**

*Materials:* paper bowls, poster paint or acrylic paint, white acrylic paint, paintbrush, pencil, scissors, glue, felt or craft foam, pom-poms, yarn

*Directions:*

1. Position a bowl bottom side up. Starting from the center, draw vertical lines to divide the bowl into an even number of sections (four or six sections will do).
2. Paint the sections alternately with two colors of poster paint. When you're done painting, set the bowl aside to dry.
3. Cut a 1.5- to 2-inch-wide strip of felt or craft foam to go around the base of the hat.
4. When the paint on the paper bowl is dry, apply glue around the base and attach the strip of felt or foam.
5. Glue a pom-pom on top of the hat.

# 27
# Holidays and Celebrations

. . . . . . . . . . . . . . . . . . . . . . . . . . . . . . . . . . . . . . . . .

## Books

**254** ***Bringing in the New Year* by Grace Lin. New York: Knopf, 2008.**

As a family gets ready to celebrate the Chinese Lunar New Year, many customs and traditions are observed. But the New Year can't get started until the lucky dragon appears!

**255** ***Weddings* by Ann Morris. New York: Lothrop, Lee and Shepard, 1995.**

Simple text and gorgeous photos explore weddings all over the world. The text explains the basics of what weddings are and what they have in common worldwide, while the stunning photos clearly show the diversity of celebrations. A photo index gives cultural background.

**256** ***Shante Keys and the New Year's Peas* by Gail Piernas-Davenport. Morton Grove, IL: Whitman, 2007.**

When Grandma forgets to make lucky black-eyed peas for the New Year's celebration, Shante is sent through the neighborhood to see if anyone has extra. Along the way, she finds that different people celebrate their holidays with foods other than black-eyed peas. Share the author's note in the back of the book about lucky New Year's food traditions.

**257** ***Birthday Customs Around the World* by Sarah L. Schuette. Mankato, MN: Capstone, 2010.**

Full-color photographs and simple text introduce birthday traditions from around the world.

## Flannelboard

**258** ***¡Fiesta!*** **by Ginger Foglesong Guy. New York: HarperCollins, 1996.**

In this simple counting story, a group of children gather everything they need for a fiesta. The text introduces basic Spanish vocabulary.

## Prop Story

**259** **The Carnival Box: A Story of Haiti**

You will need two boxes decorated with tissue paper decorations; an assortment of plastic scary items such as mice, spiders, lizards, and snakes; and an assortment of cute, cuddly stuffed animals.

It was Carnival time! Emmanuel lived in Haiti, and every year at Carnival Emmanuel couldn't wait to make a *lamayote*. What's that, you say? It's a little wooden box. Every year Emmanuel would carefully decorate his box with tissue paper and paint, and then he would put a surprise inside. He would go up to people and say, "A penny a look! Who wants to see what's in the box?" Then, after he got his penny, he would open up the box and *boo!* Everyone would have a scary surprise!

One year, Emmanuel's little sister Tatiana decided that she wanted to make a *lamayote* too. "You can't do that," said Emmanuel. "*Lamayotes* are for boys!"

"I can, too!" said Tatiana. "And I will."

So Tatiana got a box and painted it and decorated it, and she put a surprise inside.

Emmanuel and Tatiana went up to their mother. "A penny a look! Who wants to see what's in the box?" said Emmanuel. "A penny a look! Who wants to see what's in the box?" said Tatiana.

"Oh, my," said their mother. "Lucky for me I have two pennies right here." She handed them over and Emmanuel lifted the cover of his box. Inside was a spider! "AHHH!" said his mother.

Then Tatiana lifted the cover of her box. Inside was a little teddy bear. "Awwww," said her mother.

"Tatiana, you did it wrong! You're supposed to have scary stuff inside!" said Emmanuel.

They went back and put new surprises in their boxes. Then they went to see their father.

"A penny a look! Who wants to see what's in the box?" said Emmanuel. "A penny a look! Who wants to see what's in the box?" said Tatiana.

"Oh, my," said their father. "Lucky for me I have two pennies right here." He handed them over and Emmanuel lifted the cover of his box. Inside was a lizard! "AHHH!" said his father.

Then Tatiana lifted the cover of her box. Inside was a little puppy. "Awwww," said her father.

"Tatiana, you did it wrong again! You're supposed to have scary stuff inside!" said Emmanuel.

They went back and put new surprises in their boxes. Emmanuel had an idea. "Hey Tatiana, want to see what's in my box? A penny a look!"

Tatiana looked at the two pennies in her hand. "Well, okay," she said. She gave Emmanuel a penny. He lifted the cover of the box. Inside was a snake!

"AHHH!" said Tatiana. Emmanuel laughed and laughed.

"Wait," said Tatiana. "Now you have to look in my box."

Emmanuel rolled his eyes. "What will it be now? A cute, fluffy bunny?" He reached for the lid of the box.

"No, no, no," said Tatiana. "A penny a look."

Emmanuel sighed and handed her a penny. Tatiana picked up the box. "Come closer," she said. Emmanuel stepped closer. "No, closer," said Tatiana. "You need to be able to see it clearly."

Emmanuel heaved a sigh and stepped closer. Tatiana opened the box and out popped . . . a furry little kitten that gave Emmanuel a great big kiss.

"AHHHHHHHHHH!" said Emmanuel.

# Fingerplays and Songs

### 260 Aloha (ah-LOE-ha) Song (to the tune of "Hello Everybody")

May 1 is Lei Day in Hawaii. People wear flower garlands to express Hawaii's spirit of friendship and love. The word *aloha*, which is Hawaiian for "hello," "good-bye," and "I love you," expresses that same spirit.

Aloha, everybody,
Aloha to you, aloha to you, aloha to you.
Aloha everybody,
It means hello.
Aloha to you today.

Aloha, everybody,
Aloha to you, aloha to you, aloha to you.
Aloha everybody,
It means I love you.
Aloha to you today.

Aloha, everybody,
Aloha to you, aloha to you, aloha to you.
Aloha everybody,
It means good-bye.
Aloha to you today.

**261** *Imieniny* **(eem-YA-nee-nih) / Polish Name Day**

Today is my Name Day, it's my special day of the year.
In Poland on my Name Day, friends stop by to wish good cheer.
My Name Day is not my birthday, so let's not be confused.
A Name Day is when we celebrate the name given to you.
Each day on the Polish calendar a different name is listed.
So check the calendar for the date you are most gifted.

Friends and family will stop by
To wish you "*Wszystkiego najlepszego!*" (fshist-KEH-go nye-lep-SHEH-go)
That means "All the Best!"
Some will say "*Sto lat!*" (stall-lat)
That means "A hundred years!"
So thank your wonderful guests.

**262** *Five Chinese Dragons* (to the tune of "Ten Green Bottles")

5 Chinese dragons in the parade,
5 Chinese dragons in the parade,
1 got tired and flew away,
Now there are 4 Chinese dragons in the parade.

4 Chinese dragons . . .
3 Chinese dragons . . .
2 Chinese dragons . . .
1 Chinese dragon . . .

# Craft

**263** *Papel Picado*

This paper decoration found in Mexican marketplaces is often used to celebrate religious festivals and national holidays.

*Materials:* tissue paper, scissors, yarn, glue

*Directions:*

1. Accordion-fold a sheet of tissue paper.
2. Cut shapes in the folds of the tissue paper.
3. Open the paper flat, then fold over the top edge.
4. Lay yarn in the fold and glue the top edge down.

# 28

# Houses and Homes

• • • • • • • • • • • • • • • • • • • • • • • • • • • •

## Books

**264** *If You Lived Here: Houses of the World* by Giles Laroche. New York: Houghton Mifflin, 2011.

Through stunningly intricate cut-paper illustrations, this book invites readers to imagine what it would be like to live in sixteen different kinds of houses from around the world, including a Turkish yurt, a Swiss chalet, and a South African decorated house. The main text describes the experience of living in each house, while additional notes on each page tell more about each type of home and how it was constructed.

**265** *Houses and Homes* by Ann Morris. New York: Lothrop, Lee and Shepard, 1992.

Simple text and colorful photos explore homes around the world. The text examines all the things homes have in common, and a pictorial index identifies the location of each home pictured. After reading the story, go through the pictures again and ask the children to identify ways the homes pictured are similar to and different from their own.

**266** *"The Clay Pot"* from *Babushka's Mother Goose* by Patricia Polacco. New York: Penguin, 1995.

In this Russian folktale, a lonely fly makes his home in a clay pot and invites every animal that comes along to join him. When he invites a bear in, however, disaster ensues.

**267** *The Little, Little House* by Jessica Souhami. London: Frances Lincoln, 2005.

In this retelling of a Jewish folktale from Ukraine, Joseph asks the wise woman in the village to tell him how to live in a little house.

# Flannelboards

### 268 The Hare and the Lion: A Tale from Zanzibar

Adapted from a story in *Swahili Tales as Told by Natives of Zanzibar* by Edward Steere (London: Bell and Daldy, 1870).

This story could also be presented as a prop story, using lion and hare puppets and a dollhouse or a house made from a box.

Hare: Hello! I'm a hare. I look a little like a rabbit, but I am bigger and faster than a rabbit. You might have heard of my cousin, who raced with the tortoise? Well, I haven't raced with any tortoises, but I am running from a lion! He's a big, mean lion, and, well, I guess he doesn't like it very much when I play tricks on him. But you should have seen him when I squirted water in his face while he was drinking in the river! Ha ha ha! Anyway, I'm tired from playing tricks, so I'm going to go home and take a nap. See? There's my house right there. If you see the lion coming, will you warn me? How about this—if you see him coming, you tweet like a bird, and then I'll know to run! Thanks! (*Hare stifles yawn.*) Naptime! (*Place hare in house.*)

Lion: Hey, have you seen a hare come by here? He's a tricky little fellow. Wait, is that his house there? All right, now I'm going to get him! (*Prompt children to warn the hare if necessary. After they have warned him, make the hare sneak out of the house.*)

Lion (*approaching house and knocking on door*): Hmmm. Looks like the hare's not home. He's probably off playing tricks on other animals. I know! I'll wait inside until he comes home, and then I'll jump out and eat him. Then he won't be able to play tricks anymore! (*Lion goes inside house.*)

(*Show sun moving across sky.*) The sun rose higher in the sky, and the day was passing by.

Hare: Whew, I just had a great swim in the river. Now, I really need to get home and take a nap. I'm sure that silly old lion is gone by now, isn't he? (*The children will probably be happy to tell the hare that the lion is not gone, but if they don't, have the hare ask them questions until they do.*) He's still here? Hiding in the house? Well, of all the mean tricks. That's okay, I know what to do. Watch this. (*Hare approaches house.*) *Salaam*, house. *Salaam*, house! (*Hare looks expectantly at house.*) Hmm, that's strange. Every day as I come home, I say, "*Salaam*, house"—that's how you say "hello" in Swahili—and my house answers me if it is empty, but today perhaps there is someone inside it.

Lion (*inside house*): *Salaam*, Hare!

Hare: Oh, Lion, do you think I am a fool? Whoever heard of a house talking? Now I know you are in there! (*Hare dashes away.*)

Lion (*coming out of house*): I'll get that tricky hare yet! (*Lion dashes after hare.*)

And the lion is still chasing the hare to this day!

### 269 The House for Me Guessing Game

I live in the north amid ice and snow.
I stay bundled up wherever I go.
My house is made of ice block, you can come in too!
The house for me is called an . . . (igloo)!

I live in the desert where it's dry and hot.
We move around quite a lot.
If we're not there when you come, we already went.
The house for me is called a . . . (tent)!

My house has walls of solid stone.
Inside I sit upon a throne.
For you I'll lower the drawbridge without any hassle.
The house for me is called a . . . (castle)!

In my home made of mud and sticks and grass,
The windows are open, I have no glass.
It may be small, but no matter what,
The house for me is called a . . . (hut)!

In times gone by I lived with my tribe
On the Great Plains in my house made of hide.
With poles to hold it up, I didn't need a key.
The house for me was called a . . . (tepee)!

I live in a building that reaches to the sky.
Use the steps or elevator; it's many stories high.
Come into the rooms I rent.
The house for me is called an . . . (apartment)!

I live in the mountains way up high.
My home has a roof that slopes to the sky.
Inside is where I work and play.
The house for me is called a . . . (chalet)!

I don't live on the land, I live on the sea.
A traveling home is the one for me.
With my home I like to float.
The house for me is called a . . . (houseboat)!

# Fingerplays and Songs

### 270  There Was a Crooked Man: A Traditional Rhyme from England

There was a crooked man and he walked a crooked mile,
He found a crooked sixpence upon a crooked stile.
He bought a crooked cat, which caught a crooked mouse,
And they all lived together in a little crooked house.

### 271  *There Was a Little Mouse: A Rhyme from Sweden (adapted traditional)

There was a little mouse
Who wanted to come in the house.
Not here, not there,
But there! Squeak!

Try this as a partner fingerplay. One child places her fingertips together to make the shape of the house. The other child extends an index finger to represent the mouse. During the rhyme the mouse should scurry around the house looking for ways in. On "But there!" the child playing the house should gently close her hands, trapping the mouse inside. Repeat so that each child has a turn at each part.

### 272  Marching Around the House (to the tune of "The Farmer in the Dell")

Let's march around the house.
Let's march around the house.
Houses are places to live.
Let's march around the house.

Let's open up the door.
Let's open up the door.
Houses are places to live.
Let's open up the door.

In Spain, a house is called "*la casa*" (la KAH-sah)!

Let's march around *la casa*.
Let's march around *la casa*.
*Casas* are places to live.
Let's march around *la casa*.

Let's tiptoe up the stairs.
Let's tiptoe up the stairs.
Houses are places to live.
Let's tiptoe up the stairs.

In France, the word for house is "*la maison*" (la may-ZONE)!

Let's march around *la maison*.
Let's march around *la maison*.
*Les maisons* are places to live.
Let's march around *la maison*.

Let's run down the hall.
Let's run down the hall.
Houses are places to live.
Let's run down the hall.

In German, the word for house is "*das Haus*" (DAHS HOUSE)!

Let's march around *das Haus*.
Let's march around *das Haus*.
*Das Hauser* are places to live.
Let's march around *das Haus*.

Let's jump back down the stairs.
Let's jump back down the stairs.
Houses are places to live.
Let's jump back down the stairs.

In American Sign Language, this is how you say HOUSE.

Let's march around the HOUSE.
Let's march around the HOUSE.
HOUSES are places to live.
Let's march around the HOUSE.

Let's march around the house.
Let's march around the house.
Houses are places to live.
Let's march around the house.

# Craft

### 273 Native American Tepee

*Materials:* construction paper, three craft sticks, yarn, tepee wall (from template on website) cut from brown paper, crayons, markers

*Directions:*

1. Glue one craft stick vertically onto the construction paper.
2. Glue the other two craft sticks so that they overlap diagonally with the first, forming the sticks that will poke out of the top of the tepee.
3. Cut the tepee walls on the dotted lines to form an opening for the door. Fold the door flaps up.
4. Line the craft sticks with glue.
5. Place the tepee wall over the craft sticks and press down.
6. Decorate the tepee and background using crayons or markers.

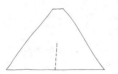

# 29

# Jungle Animals

. . . . . . . . . . . . . . . . . . . . . . . . . . . . . . . . . . .

## Books

**274** *Anansi and the Talking Melon* **by Eric A. Kimmel. New York: Holiday House, 1994.**

African folktale trickster Anansi the spider tricks all the animals in the jungle into thinking a melon can talk in this funny tale.

**275** *Tiger Tiger* **by Dee Lillegard. New York: Putnam, 2002.**

In Southeast Asia, Pocu wanders into the jungle on a hot afternoon and creates a tiger using a magic feather. But when the tiger wants to attack his village, Pocu must use the feather to wipe away his imaginary creation.

**276** *\*So Say the Little Monkeys* **by Nancy Van Laan. New York: Atheneum, 1998.**

Tiny monkeys are busy playing in the Brazilian rain forest. When the rain begins, they realize they should have taken time to build a house.

**277** *Seven Blind Mice* **by Ed Young. New York: Philomel, 1992.**

In this Indian fable, seven blind mice try to figure out what the large Something by their pond Is. Each of the first six mice makes a guess by feeling only a part of the Something, until the last mouse takes the time to feel the whole Something and realizes that it is an elephant.

# Flannelboards

### 278  Morning at the Watering Hole

The animals on the savanna begin to wake,
They walk to the watering hole with a yawn and a shake.
Hippo arrives first with a swish of his tail,
He nibbles grass along the way, moving as slow as a snail.

Quick hooves stampeding down to the hole,
The zebras arrive and take control.
Elephant comes with a trumpet and stomp,
Into the watering hole he'll play and romp.

Giraffe with his long legs approaches a bit slower,
To reach the water, he has to bend his neck lower.
Finally the monkeys come running with a squeak,
Drinking water quickly, then off to play hide and seek.

Want to see what life is like at a watering hole? Visit www.AfriCam.com.

### 279  *Little Monkey and the Bananas: A Tale from Central Africa

Based on a story in *Ten Small Tales* retold by Celia Barker Lottridge (New York: Margaret K. McElderry, 1994).

Deep in the jungle lived Little Monkey. He was naughty and loved to play tricks. But most of all he loved to eat bananas, all day long. There were plenty of bananas in the jungle, but there weren't many opportunities to play tricks. That's why, one day, he went to the human village.

He saw the houses and gardens of that village, and he longed to dance on the rooftops, and overturn the stewpots, and eat the bananas in the people's gardens. A little girl came out into her garden and saw Little Monkey. "Go away!" she said. "Unless you want to end up in someone's stewpot."

Little Monkey hadn't thought about that. How could he play his tricks if the people would catch him and eat him? So he visited Old Porcupine, who was the wisest animal in the jungle.

"Old Porcupine, I need your help," he said. "I want to go to the human village. Can you make me a magic charm so that the people won't catch me?"

Old Porcupine thought for a long moment, and then he said, "Yes, I can, Little Monkey. But you will need to do exactly as I tell you."

"I will," said Little Monkey. "Oh, thank you so much!"

So Old Porcupine mixed some bark and some roots and some leaves, and he chanted some magic words, and he made a charm for Little Monkey. He tied it around Little Monkey's neck and said, "The people will not be able to catch you, as long as you remember one thing: do not eat any bananas in the village."

"What? No bananas?" cried Little Monkey.

"No bananas," said Old Porcupine firmly. "If you eat the village bananas, you will get caught. You can eat all the bananas you want in the jungle, but you must eat none in the village."

"Very well," said Little Monkey. "I can still play my naughty tricks there!"

Little Monkey hurried to the village. He couldn't decide which prank to play first. But then he saw a garden with a beautiful banana tree. And hanging right at the top was a bunch of beautiful bananas.

Little Monkey looked at the bananas. Were they ripe? They looked nice and yellow, but they were so far away he couldn't be sure. He wanted to smell them and see if they were ripe. But he wanted to make sure he followed Old Porcupine's directions.

He ran back to Old Porcupine. "I found a big bunch of bananas. I know I can't eat them, but can I just smell them to see if they are ripe?" he asked.

Old Porcupine sighed. "Remember, I said you cannot *eat* the bananas. Anything else is up to you."

Little Monkey nodded and hurried back to the garden. He climbed up the tree and smelled each banana. They smelled sweet and ripe. Still, he knew that they might look ripe and smell ripe, but maybe if he touched them they would not feel ripe. But he wasn't sure if he should touch the bananas.

He ran back to Old Porcupine. "I smelled the bananas, but I am still not sure if they are ripe. May I touch them?" he asked.

Old Porcupine sighed. "Remember, I said you cannot *eat* the bananas. Anything else is up to you."

Little Monkey raced back to the tree and climbed up to the top. He felt each banana all over. They all felt perfectly ripe. But still Little Monkey was not sure. A banana might look ripe and smell ripe and feel ripe, but maybe if he wrapped his tongue around it, it would not taste ripe. But he wanted to make sure he didn't do the wrong thing, so he went back to Old Porcupine.

"I know I can't eat the bananas, but can I just taste one, just wrap my tongue around it to make sure it is ripe?"

Old Porcupine sighed. "Remember, I said you cannot *eat* the bananas. Anything else is up to you."

So Little Monkey hurried back to the tree. He climbed up and peeled one banana. Carefully he wrapped his tongue around it and, sure enough, it was ripe. It smelled and felt and tasted so good that Little Monkey took a bite, and that banana went right down his throat. Before he knew it, he had eaten all the bananas and fell asleep right at the top of the tree.

The little girl came out and found him there. "Oh, Little Monkey," she said. "Are you trying to end up in a stewpot?"

Little Monkey woke up and looked down at the girl. He remembered what Old Porcupine had told him, and he looked down and saw the pile of banana peels below the tree. He jumped up and ran away into the jungle.

So Little Monkey never did dance on the roofs or overturn stewpots. He decided to stay in the jungle where he could eat all the bananas he wanted without any trouble.

# Fingerplays and Songs

### 280 Savanna Ruckus

It's noisy on the savanna today,
All the animals came out to play.
The monkeys scratch their heads with an oo and an ee,
While the elephants trumpet and stomp their feet.

Hippo's tail moves with a swish, swish, swish,
While the snakes slither with a hiss, hiss, hiss.
Giraffe's neck reaches in the trees for lunch,
While the alligator waits to *snap* and munch.

### 281 *"Mbube"* by Ladysmith Black Mambazo, from *Animal Playground.* New York: Putumayo World Music, 2007.

Better known as "The Lion Sleeps Tonight," this traditional African lullaby receives a beautiful treatment in this version. Best of all, this version is slow and simple enough to sign with children. For the vocal interludes between the verses, invite the children to sign JUNGLE and make their trees sway in the wind.

In the JUNGLE, the mighty JUNGLE,

The LION SLEEPS TONIGHT.

HUSH, my darling, don't FEAR, my darling . . .

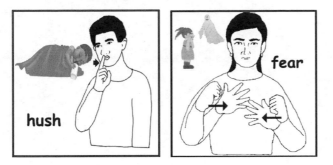

Shake your head while signing FEAR to make it mean "don't fear."

**282** **"No More Monkeys" by Asheba, from *Animal Playground*. New York: Putumayo World Music, 2007.**

This lively version of "Five Little Monkeys" by Asheba of Trinidad is a great activity song with an authentic Trinidad sound.

# Craft

**283** **Gorilla**

The gorilla is the largest primate. Some of the males weigh as much as six hundred pounds. The gorilla makes its home in African forests.

*Materials:* gorilla coloring sheet (from website), torn pieces of construction paper in various shades of green, glue, crayons

*Directions:*

1. Color the gorilla.
2. Glue torn pieces of green construction paper on the picture to create the forest leaves.

# 30
# Music and Dance

· · · · · · · · · · · · · · · · · · · · · · · · · · · · · · · · · · · · · · · · · · · · · · · · ·

## Books

**284** *Drumbeat in Our Feet* **by Patricia A. Keeler. New York: Lee and Low, 2006.**

African American children learn the dances of their African ancestors. Many different types of African dances and instruments are explained in the easy picture book format. The author provides additional information in a sidebar on each page. Vivid pictures help the reader imagine what it would be like to take part in an African dance.

**285** *\*Kitchen Dance* **by Maurie J. Manning. New York: Clarion, 2008.**

A boy and girl awake in the night to the sounds of music and dancing in the kitchen. They tiptoe downstairs to find their father singing a Spanish song into a wooden spoon and their mother dancing around, clearing dishes. The book includes many Spanish phrases and mentions many Latino foods.

**286** *Moses Goes to a Concert* **by Isaac Millman. New York: Farrar, Straus and Giroux, 1998.**

Moses, who is deaf, attends a concert with his friends and meets the percussionist from the orchestra, who is deaf herself. Throughout the story, pictures of Moses signing teach some basic phrases in American Sign Language. Kids will be fascinated at the ways the deaf characters enjoy music through vibrations—the percussionist performs barefoot, and the children hold balloons in their laps to feel the music better.

**287** *Jingle Dancer* **by Cynthia Leitich Smith. New York: Morrow, 2000.**

Jenna, who is Native American, desperately wants to dance at the powwow, but there is not enough time to order the four rows of jingles for her dress. She visits her aunt, cousin, neighbor, and grandmother and asks each for a single row of jingles from her own jingle-dancing dress. They give her the jingles, and Jenna is able to dance for all of them at the powwow.

# Flannelboard

### 288  The Bremen Town Musicians: A Folktale from Germany

Once there was a donkey who had worked for many years carrying sacks for his master. Over time the donkey grew old, and he was no longer able to work. The master decided that he wouldn't feed a donkey who no longer worked, so the donkey ran away and started off for the town of Bremen, where he could become a musician.

Along the way, the donkey met a dog lying in the road. "I am getting old," moaned the dog. "My master won't feed me anymore, because I can't work, so I ran away."

"Come with me to Bremen!" said the donkey. "I will play the lute, and you can play the drums, and the people will love us and give us food!"

So off they went. Along the way they came upon a cat. "I am getting old," moaned the cat. "My master won't feed me anymore, because I can't catch mice, so I ran away."

"Come with us to Bremen!" said the donkey. "I will play the lute, and the dog can play the drums, and you can shake a bell, and the people will love us and give us food!"

So off they went. Soon the three came upon a rooster sitting on a gate. "I am too loud," moaned the rooster. "My master won't feed me anymore because I am too noisy, so I ran away."

"Come with us to Bremen!" said the donkey. "I will play the lute, and the dog can play the drums, and the cat can shake a bell, and you can sing, and the people will love us and give us food!"

Soon day turned to night, and the four realized they should rest and continue on to Bremen the next day. The rooster noticed a light burning in a house not too far away. They went to the house hoping to rest for the night in a safe place, but when they looked in the window . . .

"Hee haw!" cried the donkey. "Look at all that gold!"

There were piles of gold and heaps of food on the table, and surely they didn't belong to the four little men who sat there, counting the gold with robbers' masks on their faces.

The animals discussed how they might drive the robbers away and made a plan. The donkey stood by the window. The dog climbed up on the donkey's back. The cat climbed onto the dog, and the rooster sat on the cat's head. Then they began to make music all together. The donkey brayed, the dog barked, the cat meowed, and the rooster crowed! (*Invite the children to make these sounds as loudly as they can.*) Then they crashed through the window. The robbers jumped up in fear that a ghost was coming and fled into the woods.

Soon the four friends were comfortable in the house and enjoying the leftover food. And the four were so happy there that they never did go to Bremen!

# Fingerplays and Songs

### 289  Zuni Harvest Dance

The Zuni tribe makes its home in New Mexico and Arizona.

We dance in a circle and clap our hands,
We dance to honor our family and lands.
We sing loud and clear, and shout through the night,
"The harvest is in!" we sing with delight.

We dance in a circle and raise our hands high,
We stand on tiptoe and reach for the sky.
We dance to the left and we dance to the right,
"The harvest is in!" we sing with delight.

We dance in a circle and jump all around,
We jump till our bodies collapse on the ground.
We danced and we sang all through the night,
The harvest is in! It's time to say goodnight.

### 290  *Dance, Children, Dance! A Rhyme from Germany (adapted traditional)

Dance, children, dance about! (*dance*)
Let your shoes in and out. (*kick up feet*)
If one should break, then we don't care. (*wrench fists apart to show breaking shoe*)
The cobbler will make you another pair. (*mime hammering on shoe*)
So dance, children, dance! (*dance*)

Now dance fast!

Repeat rhyme at fast pace.

Now dance slowly!

Repeat rhyme in slow motion.

### 291  "Mi Cuerpo Hace Musica / My Body Makes Music" from *El Doble de Amigos / Twice as Many Friends* by Sol y Canto. Cambridge, MA: Rounder Kids, 2003.

This bilingual English/Spanish CD provides wonderful dancing music with shakers and rhythm sticks, or just follow the directions and sing along.

### 292  "Mexican Hat Dance" from *Put On Your Dancing Shoes* by Joanie Bartels. Los Angeles: Purple Frog Records, 2001.

The Mexican Hat Dance is the official dance of Mexico. Place hats around the floor and have the children dance around them with maracas and other instruments.

# Craft

### 293 *Guiro*

A *guiro* is a Puerto Rican instrument, typically made from a gourd.

*Materials:* one 16-ounce empty water bottle (the kind with ridges works best), acrylic paint, paintbrush, markers, stickers, craft stick

*Directions:*

1. Remove the label from the empty water bottle.
2. Using colors of your choice, paint horizontal stripes on the clean, dry water bottle. Allow to dry and apply a second coat of paint.
3. If paint is too messy, use markers and stickers to decorate the bottle instead.
4. To play your *guiro*, use the craft stick to tap different places on the bottle or run the stick up and down along the bottle.

# 31
# My Body

## Books

**294** ***I Lost My Tooth in Africa*** **by Penda Diakité. New York: Scholastic, 2006.**

While visiting relatives in Africa, Amina loses her tooth. This book discusses a range of customs in the Mali culture, including receiving a chicken when you lose a tooth! After reading the story, ask the children what they noticed in the book that was different from what they experience here. Ask them to describe their traditions when losing a tooth.

**295** ***Tooth on the Loose*** **by Susan Middleton Elya. New York: Putnam, 2008.**

A young girl has a loose tooth, and she tries everything to get it to fall out so she will have money to buy her papa a present for his birthday. With a rhyming text interspersed with Spanish words, this book reminds us that the gift doesn't matter as much as the thought.

**296** ***The Happiest Tree: A Yoga Story*** **by Uma Krishnaswami. New York: Lee and Low, 2005.**

Meena, a girl from India, feels she is too clumsy to be even a tree in the school play. Though her parents explain that she feels clumsy because her arms and legs are growing so quickly, she still feels awkward. However, after taking yoga classes, Meena becomes a tree unlike any of the others. After reading, discuss what yoga is and practice some of the poses demonstrated at the end of the book.

**297** ***My Nose, Your Nose*** **by Melanie Walsh. New York: Houghton Mifflin, 2002.**

With straightforward language and bright, bold illustrations, this picture book examines the ways that we are all different, yet all the same. The details are rooted in a child's world—though two boys have different colors and textures of hair, neither one of them likes shampoo, and no matter what color your eyes, you close them when you go to sleep. Follow up with "Head, Shoulders, Knees, and Toes."

# Flannelboard

### 298 The Five Senses

Introduce the following Spanish words for the senses, showing the picture with the word for the sense underneath.

> sight: *vista* (VEES-tah)
> smell: *olfato* (ole-FAH-toe)
> hearing: *oído* (oh-EE-doe)
> touch: *toque* (TOH-kay)
> taste: *sabor* (sah-BORE)

Play a game asking students to say in Spanish which of their senses they use for various activities. More than one sense can often be used to answer the questions.

> What sense do you use to listen to the radio?
> What sense do you use to check for stinky sneakers?
> What sense do you use when you are eating?
> What sense do you use when you're at the beach?
> What sense do you use to check whether something is too cold?

# Fingerplays and Songs

### 299 Same and Different Game

Have the children sit on the floor. Each time you make a statement, the children should jump up if it applies to them. Emphasize how this activity shows all the things we have in common, even though we may look very different. If desired, let each child take a turn making a statement.
Some sample statements:

> "I have a sister."
> "I like popcorn."
> "I have brown eyes."
> "I have a dog."
> "I like dancing."
> "I live in a house."

**300** *"Rosh, Ktefayim, Birkayim, Etzba'ot* / Head, Shoulders, Knees, and Toes" from *Teach Me . . . Everyday Hebrew,* volume 1 (book and CD) by Judy Mahoney. Minnetonka, MN: Teach Me Tapes, 2008.

Teach the Hebrew words for the body parts, and then invite the kids to join in on this favorite song.

**301** *"Chay Chay Koolay"* from *Bridges Across the World: A Multicultural Songfest* by Sarah Barchas. Sonoita, AZ: High Haven Music, 1999.

This traditional call-and-response African folk song describes a child's morning routines and lends itself to acting out the lines.

# Craft

### 302  My Body, *Mi Cuerpo*

*Materials:* My Body, *Mi Cuerpo* worksheet (from website), crayons

*Directions:*

1. Draw a line to match each Spanish word to the body part it describes.
2. Color the picture as desired.

# My Body, *Mi Cuerpo*
Draw a line to match each set of English and Spanish words
to the body parts they describe.

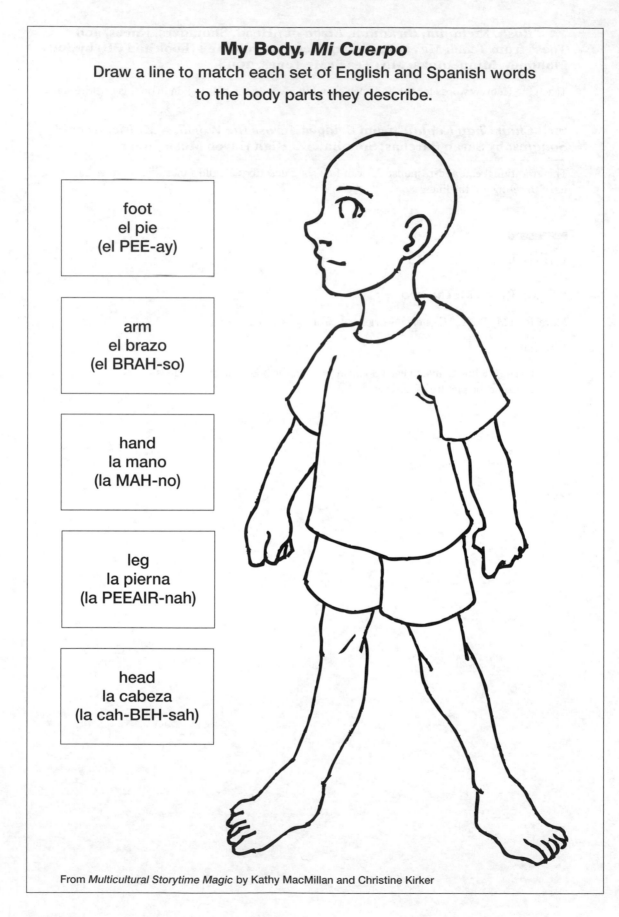

foot
el pie
(el PEE-ay)

arm
el brazo
(el BRAH-so)

hand
la mano
(la MAH-no)

leg
la pierna
(la PEEAIR-nah)

head
la cabeza
(la cah-BEH-sah)

*From Multicultural Storytime Magic by Kathy MacMillan and Christine Kirker*

# 32

# My Neighborhood

## Books

**303** ***Be My Neighbor*** **by Maya Ajmera and John D. Ivanko. Watertown, MA: Charlesbridge, 2005.**

Gorgeous full-color illustrations explore neighborhoods around the world. For storytime, read only the large text on each page. Then, if desired, share some of the more detailed information in the small text as the children look at the pictures.

**304** ***\*El Barrio*** **by Debbi Chocolate. New York: Henry Holt, 2009.**

A boy explores the streets, buildings, and special places that make up his neighborhood as his sister prepares to celebrate her *quinceañera* (fifteenth birthday). Use the glossary in the back of the book to review the Spanish terms. Ask the children to describe some of the things that make their neighborhoods special.

**305** ***For You Are a Kenyan Child*** **by Kelly Cunnane. New York: Atheneum, 2006.**

The text invites readers to imagine they are the Kenyan boy in the pictures and explore the village throughout the day.

**306** ***Jonathan and His Mommy*** **by Irene Smalls. New York: Little, Brown, 1992.**

Jonathan, an African American boy, and his mom take their daily walk through the busy city. As they proceed, they walk, run, zigzag, and more through the streets.

# Flannelboard

### 307 **It Takes a Village**

Adapted from the book by Jane Cowan-Fletcher (New York: Scholastic, 1994).

Yemi and Kokou lived in a small village in Benin. That's in Africa. It was market day, so they went with their mama to sell her mangos. Yemi and Kokou decided to look around on their own. They visited a lady selling rice because they were hungry. When they were thirsty, they visited a woman ladling water out of a gourd to drink. They talked to a man decorating gourds. When they were hot, they splashed in the river where the women were washing their clothes. When they were tired they took a nap on a sleep mat. Finally they went back to where their mother was selling mangos. They were afraid she would be worried, but she wasn't. She knew that they weren't alone and that it takes a village to raise children.

# Fingerplays and Songs

### 308 **Desaku, My Village: A Rhyme from Indonesia** (adapted traditional)

Have the children pair off and make houses out of their raised hands. Give each pair a chance to weave in and out of the houses in the "village" as you recite this rhyme.

Desaku, my sweet village,
My home which I love.
My mommy and daddy and family are all there.
I will not forget it,
I don't want to leave it.
I will always love it,
Desaku, my sweet home.

**309** **At the End of the Village: A Rhyme from Serbia** (adapted traditional)

At the end of the village stands a yellow house, (*clasp hands together so that fingers form roof of house*)
A yellow house, a little yellow house.
Inside lives a mother, an old mother, (*turn hands so that clasped fingers face listeners and raise one thumb, bent slightly, to be the mother*)
A little old mother.
She has one daughter, one sweet daughter, (*raise other thumb to be the daughter*)
One sweet little daughter.
The daughter has working hands, (*wiggle "daughter" thumb to show working*)
Helping hands, helping, working hands.
They live in the village in the yellow house, (*turn hands so that roof points up and tuck mother and daughter into house*)
The yellow house, the little yellow house.

**310** **\*My Neighborhood: A Song in ASL and English** (to the tune of "The Wheels on the Bus")

At the LIBRARY I read, read, read,
Read, read, read,
Read, read, read.
At the LIBRARY I read, read, read,
It's in my town.

I go to the market (STORE) to shop, shop, shop . . .
I go to SCHOOL to learn, learn, learn . . .
At the HOSPITAL they help me get well . . .

# Craft

### 311  Huichol Yarn Painting

Huichol Indians of Mexico are known for their yarn paintings. Traditionally, the Huichol use beeswax melted in the sun and spread over a piece of wood. They then push yarn into the wax to create images.

*Materials:* yarn in a variety of colors, scissors, glue, construction paper, pencil

*Directions:*

1. Use the pencil to draw the outlines of buildings on the construction paper. (Alternately, you could provide a simple picture of a neighborhood.)
2. Run glue over the outlines of the picture.
3. Cut yarn to appropriate lengths and place it along the glue lines.

# 33 Nature

........................................................

## Books

**312** ***Koi and the Kola Nuts*** **by Verna Aardema. New York: Atheneum, 1999.**

The value of kindness is the theme of this Liberian folktale. Koi inherits only a little kola tree when his father, a great headman, dies. But when he shares the nuts of the tree with those he meets as he journeys through the world, he makes valuable friends who come to his aid and help him win a beautiful wife.

**313** ***The Great Kapok Tree*** **by Lynne Cherry. New York: Harcourt, 1990.**

Many eyes watch nervously as a man enters the Amazon rain forest to chop down a great kapok tree. When he grows tired and takes a nap, snakes, bees, monkeys, birds, frogs, and even a jaguar emerge from the jungle canopy to plead with him to spare their home. When the man awakens, startled at all the rare and marvelous animals surrounding him, he experiences a change of heart and leaves the tree alone.

**314** ***\*Pablo's Tree*** **by Pat Mora. New York: Simon and Schuster, 1994.**

When Pablo's mother adopted him as a baby, his *abuelito* (grandfather) planted a special tree in his yard. Each year Abuelito decorates the tree with surprises for Pablo's birthday. This touching story presents the concept of adoption in a straightforward, easy-to-understand way and incorporates basic Spanish phrases.

**315** ***Giving Thanks: A Native American Good Morning Message*** **by Chief Jake Swamp. New York: Lee and Low, 1995.**

Based on the Thanksgiving Address, a traditional Iroquois message of peace, this gentle book encourages appreciation of Mother Earth and all Earth's creatures.

# Flannelboard

### 316 *The Bossy Rooster: A Folktale from Cuba

Rooster was so excited. Today was his uncle's wedding! He combed his feathers carefully and set off down the road. He did not want to be late. He thought about all the delicious food that would be at the wedding feast, and he started to grow hungry. "Why didn't I eat breakfast?" he said to himself. He began to look around him for something to eat. But all he found was a kernel of corn in the middle of a mud puddle. "I can't eat that corn!" he thought. "My beak will get dirty, and then I will be a disgrace when I show up at my uncle's wedding."

But his stomach growled and growled and he couldn't stop looking at that corn. Finally he could stand it no more—he leaned forward and ate up that corn. And his beak was covered with mud!

He looked around and saw the grass on the side of the road. "Oh, grass, dear grass," he said, "please clean my beak so that I can go to my uncle's wedding."

But the grass said, "No, why should I?"

Rooster saw a lamb grazing in the field. He had an idea. He said to the lamb, "Oh, lamb, dear lamb, please eat the grass so it will be scared into cleaning my beak so that I can go to my uncle's wedding."

But the lamb said, "No, why should I?"

Rooster frowned. He went over to a stick lying in the road, and said to it, "Stick, dear stick, please hit the lamb so it will eat the grass so it will be scared into cleaning my beak so that I can go to my uncle's wedding."

But the stick said, "No, why should I?"

Rooster was starting to panic. If he didn't get his beak clean soon, he would be late for the wedding! He looked around and saw a campfire that some shepherds had left. He spoke to it. "Fire, dear fire, please burn the stick so it will hit the lamb so it will eat the grass so it will be scared into cleaning my beak so that I can go to my uncle's wedding."

But the fire said, "No, why should I?"

Rooster ruffled his feathers. He went to the brook and said, "Water, dear water, please threaten to put out the fire so it will burn the stick so it will hit the lamb so it will eat the grass so it will be scared into cleaning my beak so that I can go to my uncle's wedding."

But the water said, "No, why should I?"

Poor Rooster didn't know what to do. He lifted his head and let out a "Cock-a-doodle-doo!" And at that moment the sun broke through the clouds. The rooster cried out, "Sun, dear sun, please threaten to dry out the water so that it will threaten to put out the fire so that it will threaten to burn the stick so it will hit the lamb so it will eat the grass so it will be scared into cleaning my beak so that I can go to my uncle's wedding."

And the sun said, "Of course I will, my good friend Rooster! Every morning you greet me with your lovely song. I will happily help you."

But the water cried, "Please don't dry me out. I will put out the fire."

And the fire cried, "Please don't put me out. I will burn the stick."

The stick cried, "Please don't burn me. I will hit the lamb."

The lamb cried out, "Please don't hit me. I will eat the grass."

But the grass cried, "Please don't eat me. I will clean the rooster's beak."

And so the grass cleaned Rooster's beak, and it shone in the sunlight. "Cock-a-doodle-doo! Thank you, my friends!" said Rooster. And he made it to his uncle's wedding in plenty of time!

# Fingerplays and Songs

### 317  Under the Big Chestnut Tree: A Traditional Japanese Rhyme

Pass out scarves to all the children. Ask half the children to hold their scarves up to make the branches of the tree. The other half should skip under the "tree" waving their scarves as you say the rhyme. Then have the children switch places and repeat the rhyme.

Under the big chestnut tree,
You and I play happily,
Under the big chestnut tree.

### 318  The Tree: A Rhyme in ASL and English

There was a TREE so straight and tall
People came to see it from miles around.
But one day the winds blew it to and fro (*sign* TREE *with hand moving back and forth as if in wind*)
And knocked it to the ground. (*show tree falling to ground*)
But an acorn fell off of the tree,
Tumbled to the soil, and then
The sun and rain helped it to grow, (*show tree growing*)
And a tree stood there again!

tree

### 319 *Ke Ao Nani* / This Beautiful World: A Traditional Rhyme from Hawaii

High, high above (*raise arms*)
Birds fly in the sky. (*flap arms*)
Way down below (*crouch down*)
Grow the flowers of the earth. (*lift arms and "grow" like a flower*)
Up in the mountains (*raise arms*)
Stands a grove of trees. (*stand tall like a tree*)
Swimming in the waves (*move arms like waves*)
The fishes of the ocean (*make a fish face*)
Tell the story (*spread arms*)
Of this beautiful world.
It's here for all the children. (*indicate children*)

### 320 *"Tu-tu-tu-tu"* from *Jewish Holiday Songs for Children* by Rachel Buchman. Cambridge, MA: Rounder, 1993.

This song celebrates Tu biShvat, also known as Jewish Arbor Day, but it is appropriate for any program about trees. Emphasize to the children that cultures around the world celebrate trees in different ways. The verses invite the children to act out the steps of planting a tree, from digging a hole to watering and growing.

# Craft

### 321 Native American Painting

Native Americans of the Pacific Northwest used berries to paint houses, bowls, boxes—even their faces!

*Materials:* blackberries, blueberries, raspberries, small bowls, wooden spoons, vinegar, Indian paintbrush or other types of grass, cotton swabs, paper

*Directions:*

1. Let each child have a turn mashing some berries with a wooden spoon.
2. Add a few drops of vinegar to prevent mold growth.
3. Mash the berries some more.
4. Using cotton swabs or grasses, paint designs on the paper with this natural paint. Experiment with different types of grasses to create different designs.

# 34
# Parents

## Books

**322** ***Papá and Me* by Arthur Dorros. New York: HarperCollins, 2008.**

A bilingual boy and his father, who speaks only Spanish, spend the day together in the park and eventually go to his grandfather's house.

**323** ***Papa, Do You Love Me?* by Barbara M. Joosse. San Francisco: Chronicle, 2005.**

A young Maasai boy asks his father the universal titular question, and his father answers, describing his unconditional love in the language of their everyday lives. A glossary at the back of the book offers more explanation of the Maasai culture that appears throughout the story. After reading the story, go back through the book and ask the children what some of the unfamiliar words, such as *calabash*, mean. Encourage the children to work out the meaning from the text and the pictures before you offer the explanation from the glossary.

**324** ***The Mommy Book* by Ann Morris. Parsippany, NJ: Silver Press, 1996.**

Large, color illustrations and a simple text examine the roles mothers and grandmothers play around the world. An "Index to Mommies" indicates where each picture was taken.

**325** ***On Mother's Lap* by Ann Herbert Scott. New York: Clarion, 1992.**

A young Inuit boy learns that there is always enough room on Mother's lap in this gentle, practically perfect picture book.

## Flannelboard

**326 *Mama, Do You Love Me?* by Barbara M. Joosse. San Francisco: Chronicle, 1991.**

A young Inuit girl asks her mother the universal titular question, and her mother answers, describing her unconditional love in the language of their everyday lives. A glossary at the back of the book offers more explanation of the Inuit culture that appears throughout the story.

## Fingerplays and Songs

**327 Parents Around the World**

In France, they call her *Mère*, (MARE)
In Germany she's *Mutter*, (MOO-ta)
In Spain she is a *madre*, (MAH-dray)
In Japan she is a *haha*. (ha-ha)

No matter what you call her, she's the one who loves you best.
Who is this special lady? Do you know? Can you guess? (*mother*)

In Japan he is a *chichi*, (chee-chee)
In Italy and Spain he is a *padre*, (PAH-dray)
In India he is *Pitā*, (pee-tah)
In Germany he's *Vater*. (fah-tah)

No matter what you call him, he's the guy who loves you best.
Who is this special man? Do you know? Can you guess? (*father*)

No matter what you call them, at home or far away,
Mom and Dad love their families each and every day!

### 328  *Sleep, Baby, Sleep! A Traditional German Rhyme

Sleep, baby, sleep!
Thy father guards the sheep,
Thy mother shakes the dreamland tree,
And from it fall sweet dreams for thee.
Sleep, baby, sleep!

Sleep, baby, sleep!
Across the sky roam sheep.
The stars are little baby lambs,
They're herded by the moon's kind hands.
Sleep, baby, sleep!

Sleep, baby, sleep!
To you, I'll give a sheep,
And with a little golden bell,
It'll play with you and stories tell.
Sleep, baby, sleep!

Sleep, baby, sleep!
Away now, guard the sheep,
Away with you, black sheepdog fine,
And don't you wake this baby mine!
Sleep, baby, sleep!

### 329  *Papito, Mamita: A Rhyme from Ecuador (adapted traditional)

*Papito,* my daddy,
I am so small. (*crouch down into a ball*)
But my little heart loves you (*stand up and grow*)
Biggest of all! (*spread arms wide*)

*Mamita,* my mommy,
I am so small. (*crouch down into a ball*)
But my little heart loves you (*stand up and grow*)
Biggest of all! (*spread arms wide*)

**330** **"Here Come Our Mothers" from *I Have a Dream: World Music for Children* by Daria Marmaluk-Hajioannou. Riegelsville, PA: Dariamusic, 2009.**

This traditional Zulu song tells of the time of year that the mothers sell their extra food in the markets and always bring something extra home for their children. Pass out drums, shakers, or rhythm sticks to use with this song.

# Craft

**331** **Parent's Day Card**

Parent's Day is celebrated in India on the fourth Sunday of July every year. This festival honors mothers and fathers for their devotion and sacrifices made to provide a secure and promising future for their children. On this day, children give gifts and cards to express their love and to honor their parents.

*Materials:* construction paper, crayons, glitter, scissors, glue, magazines to be cut, other items to decorate with

*Directions:*

1. Fold construction paper in half to form a card.
2. Write "Happy Parent's Day" and any other special messages on the card. This may be a good place for the children to express their appreciation for something their parents do.
3. Decorate the card as desired.

# 35 Playtime

- - - - - - - - - - - - - - - - - - - - - - - - - - - - - - -

## Books

**332 *1, 2, 3, Go!* by Huy Voun Lee. New York: Henry Holt, 2000.**

This simple counting story introduces Chinese characters for the numbers one to ten as well as action words.

**333 *Babushka's Doll* by Patricia Polacco. New York: Simon and Schuster, 1990.**

Natasha doesn't understand why her babushka (Russian for "grandmother") won't stop what she's doing and push her in the swing, make lunch, or push her in the goat cart whenever she wants. But when she gets a chance to play with Babushka's doll, who comes to life and turns out to be twice as demanding as Natasha herself, she learns a thing or two about patience and manners.

**334 *\*Snap!* by Marcia Vaughan. New York: Scholastic, 1994.**

Little Joey and his Australian animal friends find many games to play on a hot day and even find a playful way to outfox the crocodile who tries to eat them.

**335 *Galimoto* by Karen Lynn Williams. New York: HarperCollins, 1990.**

Kondi, a young boy in Malawi, is determined to find enough wire to make a *galimoto*—a toy vehicle.

# Flannelboard

### 336 **Festival of Tano**

Tano is one of Korea's holidays. Tano occurs on the fifth day of the fifth lunar month and is also known as "Swing Day" because women and girls participate in a swinging contest, where they swing standing up!

5 girls swinging on this Tano day,
1 jumped off and dashed away.
4 girls swinging having lots of fun,
1 jumped off and started to run.
3 girls swinging, back and forth they go,
1 jumped off and skipped just so.
2 girls swinging, happy as can be,
1 jumped off and said, "Look at me!"
1 girl swinging in the sun,
She jumped off and then there were none.

# Fingerplays and Songs

### 337 *Andar, Bahar*: **A Traditional Game from India**

Make a large circle on the floor using masking tape. Have the children stand outside the circle. When you say "In," the children should jump into the circle. When you say "Out," they should jump out. Begin slowly, then speed up your instructions and challenge the children to follow. If you say "In" when the children are already inside the circle, or "Out" when they are already out, they should freeze. In the traditional game, children who do not follow the directions correctly are out, but preschoolers find the game equally fun if no one goes out. For older children, make the game more challenging by teaching them the Hindi words *andar* ("in") and *bahar* ("out") and using them during the game.

### 338 **\*Swinging: A Rhyme from Japan** (adapted traditional)

Swinging, swinging high,
The sky is swinging by.
Sway and swing, sway and swing,
The treetops sway and swing.
Watch me, watch me swing!
Sway and swing, sway and swing,
Sway and swing, sway and swing,
Swinging with my friends,
Good boys and girls.
Sway and swing, sway and swing,
All swing together now, let's sway and swing!

### 339 **Millstone: A Circle Game from the Czech Republic**

This rhyme is similar to "Ring Around the Rosy." Have the children join hands in a circle. As you recite the rhyme, the children should move around in a circle. On the crash, everyone should drop to the floor. Repeat, experimenting with opposites: challenge the children to do the rhyme quickly, then slowly, then loudly, then softly.

Millstone, millstone, worth four golden coins.
It broke in half and down it fell
Onto the ground. Crash!

### 340 *"Balloon Song" from *Multicultural Children's Songs* by Ella Jenkins. Washington, DC: Smithsonian Folkways, 1995.

This simple song from India is in English, one of the official languages of India.

# Craft

### 341 *Mancala*: A Traditional Game from Africa

*Materials:* an egg carton, glue, markers or crayons, 48 pebbles (or buttons, beads, seeds, or beans)

*Directions:*

1. First, cut the lid off the egg carton. Cut the lid in half.
2. Lay the pieces of the lid in front of you with the ends touching (as if they had not been cut). Pull the two pieces of the lid away from each other 1½ inches. Glue the egg cups into the lids. This creates a tray at each end. The tray is called the *mancala*.
3. Decorate the egg cups as desired.
4. Place four pebbles, buttons, beads, seeds, or beans in each egg cup.

*How to Play* Mancala:

*Mancala* is a game for two players. The board sits between the two players with the long sides facing them. As you face the board, the six cups closest to you are yours, and your *mancala* (scoring tray) is the tray to your right. The goal is to collect as many pebbles as possible before one player empties all his or her egg cups.

1. To begin, place four pebbles, buttons, beads, seeds, or beans into each cup.
2. On your turn, pick up all the pebbles from one of your cups. One by one, put the pebbles into the cups around the board in a counterclockwise direction. Include your own *mancala* in this rotation, but not your opponent's.
3. If your last pebble lands in your *mancala*, go again.
4. If your last pebble lands in an empty cup on your own side, you may take all the pebbles from your opponent's cup directly opposite your empty cup. Place the pebbles in your *mancala*.
5. The game is over when a player has no more pebbles in the cups. The other player then takes all the pebbles left on his or her side and places them into his or her *mancala*. The player who has the most pebbles in his or her *mancala* wins!

# 36
# School Days

· · · · · · · · · · · · · · · · · · · · · · · · · · · · · · · · · · ·

## Books

### 342 *Yasmin's Hammer* by Ann Malaspina. New York: Lee and Low, 2010.

Yasmin and her family live in the crowded city of Dhaka, Bangladesh. Everyone in the family must work to put food on the table, including Yasmin and her little sister, who chip bricks for use in road building. But Yasmin has a dream—she wants to go to school and learn to read—and her passion inspires her whole family to find a way to make it happen. What could have been a bleak, depressing story instead becomes a tale of hope and triumph, thanks to the author's sensitive text and the bright, evocative illustrations.

### 343 *Moses Goes to School* by Isaac Millman. New York: Farrar, Straus and Giroux, 2000.

Moses's school is a lot like most other city public schools—except that he and his classmates are deaf, and they communicate in American Sign Language. Throughout the story, illustrations of Moses signing teach basic phrases in American Sign Language. After reading the story, invite the children to compare and contrast their own schools with Moses's school.

### 344 *\*Where Are You Going, Manyoni?* by Catherine Stock. New York: Morrow, 1993.

A little girl living near the Limpopo River in Zimbabwe sees bushpigs, impala, and other sights of the plains on her way to school.

### 345 *Yoko Writes Her Name* by Rosemary Wells. New York: Hyperion, 2008.

Yoko can write her name beautifully in Japanese. Most of her classmates want to learn to write their names in Japanese, too—all except Olive and Sylvia, who tease Yoko that her writing is "only scribbling." But on the last day of kindergarten, when everyone else in the class can write their names in English *and* Japanese, the two girls panic—until Yoko's kindness saves the day.

# Flannelboard

### 346  Going to School

Introduce the following Spanish vocabulary, then give the clues below and ask the children to name the school item being described.

> school: *escuela* (es-KOAY-lah)
> desk: *el escritorio* (el es-cree-TOE-ree-o)
> pencil: *el lápiz* (el LA-peess)
> notebook: *el cuaderno* (el coo-ah-DER-no)

*Clues:*

> I go here to learn.
> This is where we sit when we go to school.
> We use this to write with.
> We write in these.

# Fingerplays and Songs

### 347  Name the Color

Hold up squares in the following colors and teach the children the corresponding French words. Then read the rhyme below and ask the class to fill in the colors in French.

> red: *rouge* (roozh)
> blue: *bleu* (bluh)
> green: *vert* (vair)
> yellow: *jaune* (zhone)
> What is the color: *Ce qui est la couleur?* (sa key ay la koo-LOOR)

I like my teacher, he's really great,
I brought him an apple of this color which he quickly ate. *Ce qui est la couleur?*

During recess my teacher takes us outside to play,
When the sky is this color, it's a fun day! *Ce qui est la couleur?*

My teacher is better than all the rest,
Our class pet is a snake of this color, it is the best! *Ce qui est la couleur?*

I like school, but when the day is done,
I run outside to see the bus! *Ce qui est la couleur?*

**348 My School** (to the tune of "The Wheels on the Bus")

In Cambodia my school floats, floats, floats,
Floats, floats, floats,
Floats, floats, floats.
In Cambodia my school floats, floats, floats,
Because it is on water.

In Kenya my school is under a tree . . . because it gives us shade.
In India my school is in the jungle . . . on a smooth dirt floor.
In the outback my school is online . . . because we live so far away.

**349 In the Country of New Zealand** (to the tune of "When the Saints Go Marching In")

New Zealand is located in the southern hemisphere, so the seasons are the opposite of those in the northern hemisphere. December, January, and February are the summer there, and winter comes in June, July, and August. The school year is different, too, because of this. Most schools run from late January through mid-December.

Use a globe or map to show the children where New Zealand is located and explain that its seasons are the opposite of ours. Then invite the children to march with you and act out the seasons as you sing the following song. Wipe sweat from your forehead for summer, crunch the leaves in autumn, bundle up in winter, and breathe the fresh air in spring.

It's time for school! It's time for school!
In the country of New Zealand.
School begins, we're on our way,
On this warm January day.

Let's go to school! Let's go to school!
In the country of New Zealand.
In March, April, and May
We have our autumn school days.

It's getting cold! It's getting cold!
In the country of New Zealand.
Put on your hat, the wind will gust
In June, July, and August.

And now it's spring! And now it's spring!
In the country of New Zealand.
September, October, and November,
And school's out for summer in December!

# Craft

### 350 **Berry Ink**

Pokeberry ink was used by Native Americans to decorate their horses, was rumored to be the ink used to write the Declaration of Independence, and was used by soldiers during the Civil War to write letters home. As the pokeberry plant is toxic and will stain, we have replaced it in this craft with blackberries, which are easier to obtain and safer to use with children.

*Materials:* ½ cup ripe blackberries, strainer, bowl, spoon, ½ teaspoon salt, ½ teaspoon vinegar, small jar, plastic gloves, feather with quill, writing paper

*Directions:*

1. Put berries in a strainer and hold the strainer over a bowl. Crush the berries with a spoon, straining only the juice of the berries into the bowl.
2. Add ½ teaspoon salt and ½ teaspoon vinegar to the bowl with the blackberry juice and mix well. The salt will prevent the ink from spoiling, and the vinegar will help the color of the ink last longer.
3. Dip your quill in the ink and practice writing on paper.
4. Store ink in a tightly covered jar such as a small canning jar or a baby food jar when not in use.

# 37
# Shoes

## Books

**351** ***Happy Birthday, Jamela!* by Niki Daly. New York: Farrar, Straus and Giroux, 2006.**

Jamela, a little girl in South Africa, yearns for sparkly "Princess Shoes" to wear with her new birthday dress, but her mother insists on buying sturdy school shoes instead. So Jamela adds her own sparkles, infuriating her mother, until a local artist sees the shoes and works with Jamela to sell them at her stand in the market.

**352** ***The Golden Sandal: A Middle Eastern Cinderella Story* by Rebecca Hickox. New York: Holiday House, 1998.**

A magical fish helps a young Iraqi girl get to the party she so desperately wants to attend, despite her stepmother's disapproval. When, in her haste to leave before her stepmother, she loses one of her magical golden sandals in the river, the mishap leads to her surprise happy ending.

**353** ***The Legend of the Lady Slipper* by Lise Lunge-Larsen and Margi Preus. Boston: Houghton Mifflin, 1999.**

In this Ojibwa legend and pourquoi tale, a young girl travels to a neighboring village to get *mash-ki-ki*, healing herbs, for her sick neighbors. Crossing an icy river on her way back, she falls in and loses her beautiful beaded moccasins. The next spring, when she looks for her lost shoes, she finds that beautiful flowers shaped liked moccasins have sprouted everywhere she stepped on her journey home.

354 *Shoes, Shoes, Shoes* by Ann Morris. New York: Lothrop, Lee and Shepard, 1995.

Simple text and color photos explore different types of shoes around the world. The text emphasizes the commonalities, while the photos show the variety of shoes from different cultures. A photo index identifies the origins of all the shoes discussed.

# Flannelboards

## 355 The Seven Iron Slippers: A Tale from Portugal

Adapted from a story in *Portuguese Folk-tales* by Consiglieri Pedroso, Henriquetta Monteiro, William Ralston, and Shedden Ralston (Great Britain: Folklore Society, 1882).

Once upon a time there was a king who had a beautiful daughter. He loved the princess very much. When the princess became a young woman, he had a mystery on his hands—every night he would send her to bed, and every morning she would come to breakfast exhausted. When the king looked in her room, he found that during the night she had worn out not one pair but *seven* pairs of slippers. And her shoes were no ordinary shoes—they were made of iron! Each night this happened, and the king could not understand why. At last the king made an announcement that any man who could solve the mystery would marry the princess.

Now in that kingdom there was a soldier. One day he was walking along, carrying a sack of oranges, when he saw two men fighting. "What are you fighting about?" he asked them.

"We are fighting," said one man, "because our father left us this magic cap, and we both want it! If you put it on and say, 'Cap, cover me!' you become invisible."

"I see," said the soldier. "Perhaps I can help. I'll stand here with the cap, and I will throw one of my oranges. You two race after it, and whichever man touches it first shall have the cap."

The men thought this was a good idea. So the soldier took the cap and threw the orange, and as soon as the two men ran after the fruit, the soldier popped the cap on his head and said, "Cap, cover me!"

When the two men came back, the soldier was nowhere to be seen.

The soldier laughed as he slipped away. When the men were out of sight, he slipped the cap into his bag and continued down the road. A little while later he saw another two men, again fighting.

"What are you fighting about?" he asked them.

"We are fighting," said one man, "because our father left us these magic boots, and we both want them! If you put them on and tell them where you want to go, you have but to take a step, and you will be there."

"I see," said the soldier. "Perhaps I can help. I'll stand here with the boots, and I will throw one of my oranges. You two race after it, and whichever man touches it first shall have the boots."

The men thought this was a good idea. So the soldier took the boots and threw the orange, and as soon as the two men ran after the fruit, the soldier popped the cap on his head and said, "Cap, cover me!" Then he put on the boots and said, "Boots, take me to the city."

When the two men came back, the soldier was nowhere to be seen.

The soldier had indeed gone to the city. When he heard about the king's announcement, that any man who solved the mystery of the seven pairs of iron slippers should marry the princess, he decided to try his luck. After all, he had two wonderful magical tools to help him.

He presented himself to the king. "Very well, I will let you try," said the king. "But, if at the end of three days you have not solved the mystery, you shall be put to death."

So, that night, the soldier sat in the princess's bedroom to keep watch over her. She was very polite, even bringing him a cup of tea before she went to bed. The soldier did not realize that the tea contained a sleeping potion. He did not see anything that happened that night, because he slept soundly.

It happened again the second night, and when the king asked the soldier if he had seen anything, the soldier replied, "Nothing, Your Majesty. Night came and went as always." But he was starting to suspect that something was not right.

He had only one more night to solve the mystery, so on the third night, when the princess brought the soldier a cup of tea, he only pretended to drink it. He dumped it out into a potted plant when she wasn't looking, and then he pretended to go to sleep.

The princess, once she thought he was asleep, arose and put on her iron slippers. She went to the door and left. Quickly the soldier slapped on his cap and said, "Cap, cover me!" He drew on the boots and said, "Boots, take me wherever the princess goes."

The princess entered a carriage, and the soldier followed. The carriage stopped at the seashore, where the princess climbed on board a ship. They traveled for some time, until they reached the land of the giants. They left the ship and walked to a beautiful palace, where a giant's ball was in progress. The princess sat beside one of the giants. The soldier hid under their enormous chair.

Soon the princess and the giant got up to dance. When they came back, the princess's iron shoes had fallen to pieces. She took them off and shoved them under the seat. The soldier grabbed them and put them in his sack.

The next time she went to dance, the same thing happened. Again, she shoved the ruined iron slippers under her seat, and again the soldier carefully put them in his sack. Seven times she rose to dance with the giant, and seven times did she put the ruined iron slippers under her seat.

After the seventh pair of slippers went into the sack, the soldier stood behind their chair and shoved it forward, dumping both the princess and the giant onto the ground. They could not see him, of course, but the giants searched all over the palace to see which invisible spirit had gotten in.

When the princess left the land of the giants at daybreak, the soldier followed her, quiet and invisible. At breakfast that morning, the princess was quiet. She had a sore bottom from being dumped on the floor. When the king asked the soldier if he had seen anything, the soldier said, "I saw the princess fall on her rear." The princess looked at him, astonished, and she knew that he was the one who had pushed her chair and made her fall to the ground. Then the soldier pulled the seven pairs of iron slippers from his sack and said, "I believe these are yours."

The princess smiled. "You have broken the giant's spell! For two years I have been forced to go dance with him every night and could not tell anyone where I went. But now you have broken the spell and I am free!"

The king was delighted, and so was the soldier. The princess and the soldier were married the next day, and after the wedding they had a quiet sit-down party—with no dancing.

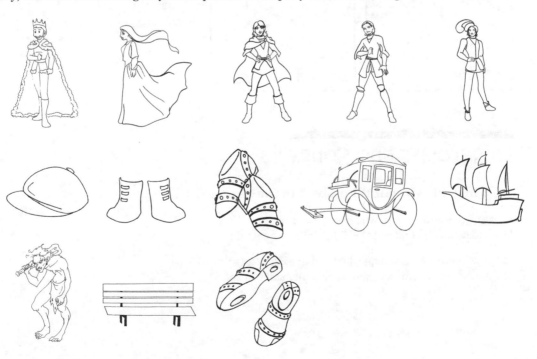

### 356 *I Like Shoes: A Rhyme in ASL and English

SHOES, SHOES, I like SHOES.
They come in WHITE and RED and BLUE,
ORANGE and GREEN and sometimes BROWN.
I wear my SHOES all over town!

To extend this activity, cut out shoe shapes in the colors mentioned in the rhyme. Teach the signs for the colors, then play a game. Place one shoe from each pair on the board, and pass the others out to the children. Then sign the colors and have the children come up to match the pairs of shoes.

# Fingerplays and Songs

### 357 The Old Woman Who Lived in the Shoe (adapted traditional)

There once was a woman who lived in a shoe.
She had so many children, she didn't know what to do.

In Spain there was a woman who lived in a *zapato*. (sah-PAH-toe)
She had so many children, she hugged them all just so!

In France there was a woman who lived in a *chaussure*. (show-SYOOR)
She had so many children, but there was always room for more!

In China there was a woman who lived in a *xi*. (shee)
She had so many children, she made them all some tea!

**358** **"Zapatos" from *El Doble de Amigos / Twice as Many Friends* by Sol y Canto. Cambridge, MA: Rounder Kids, 2003.**

This bilingual English/Spanish song provides wonderful music for dancing with maracas.

**359** **Wish on a Shoe**

In Russia, making a wish on a penny placed in your shoe is thought to bring luck.

I have a little penny,
I put it in my shoe.
Maybe you might think this is
A silly thing to do.
But I know that little penny
Has an important job to do.
I made a wish and so it will
Make that wish come true!

# Craft

**360** **Dutch Wooden Shoes**

*Materials:* two wooden shoe shapes cut from posterboard (from template on website), markers, crayons, tape, stapler, hole punch, thin elastic

*Directions:*

1. Decorate shoes as desired.
2. Staple both short ends together for the part behind the heels.
3. Fold just the tip to make the pointed end at the toes. Attach the ends together with tape.
4. Punch a hole on either side of each shoe, just in front of the heels. Pull a piece of thin elastic through each hole and tie a knot to keep it in place.
5. Pull the wooden shoes on over your feet.

# 38
# Shopping

## Books

**361** ***Baby-O* by Nancy White Carlstrom. Boston: Little, Brown, 1992.**

In this singsong story with a cumulative refrain, a West Indian family gathers together to take a trip to market.

**362** ***Mama Panya's Pancakes: A Village Tale from Kenya* by Mary and Rich Chamberlin. Cambridge, MA: Barefoot Books, 2005.**

Mama Panya has just enough money to buy ingredients for pancakes for herself and her son, so when he invites all their friends at the market, she worries that there won't be enough for everyone. But somehow with "a little bit and a little bit more," it all works out in the end.

**363** ***Market Day* by Lois Ehlert. New York: Harcourt, 2000.**

Simple rhyming text and colorful collages describe a trip to a South American market. After reading the story, discuss why market day is so important in this part of the world.

**364** ***My Father's Shop* by Satomi Ichikawa. La Jolla, CA: Kane/Miller, 2006.**

Mustafa, a young Moroccan boy, helps his father sell beautiful carpets to tourists. His father wants him to learn other languages, but Mustafa only wants to play with the damaged rug his father gave him. When he runs through the market wearing the rug and attracts a rooster, he makes new friends from many countries and learns how to "speak rooster" in five languages.

# Flannelboard

### 365 The Little Pot: A Folktale from Palestine

Adapted from *Tunjur! Tunjur! Tunjur! A Palestinian Folktale* by Margaret Read MacDonald (Tarrytown, NY: Marshall Cavendish, 2006).

Once there was a woman who had no children. One day she prayed to Allah for a child. She said, "How I would love a little child of my own, even if it was just a little cooking pot!"

Later that day, when the woman was preparing to boil some chickpeas for hummus, she took a pot from the cupboard. "Mama!" cried the pot. The woman was astonished, but so happy. At last she had a little child of her own.

All day long while the woman worked, the pot would roll around on the floor, playing. "*Tunjur! Tunjur! Tunjur!*" was the sound the little pot made as it rolled along.

One day the pot was bored. "I want to go to the market and see the world!" said the pot.

"Oh, no, little pot, I can't take you right now because I am busy, and you can't go by yourself. You are not yet old enough to know right from wrong."

But the little pot pleaded, and finally the woman decided to give her a chance.

So the little pot rolled happily to the market. But the honey seller saw the pot and said, "Oh, this little pot is perfect to fill with honey and take home to my wife!" The little pot *loved* honey, so she didn't say anything while the man filled her up with honey. But when he took the pot home to his wife, she tried to pull off the lid, and the little pot held on tight. The wife pulled and pulled, and the man pulled and pulled, but they couldn't get that lid off!

The little pot giggled and shook until they dropped her, and then she rolled back home, singing, "My mouth is full of honey! *Tunjur! Tunjur! Tunjur!*"

When the little pot arrived home, the old woman thought that the honey was a gift from the honey seller. "How kind!" she said.

The next day the pot begged to go to the market again.

"Are you sure you are old enough to know right from wrong?" said the woman.

"Yes, Mama!" said the pot.

"Very well, but be careful," said the woman.

The little pot rolled happily into town and through the marketplace. And this time she rolled right up to the palace door! The king found her lying there and said, "What a fine pot! It's just the right size for my wife to keep her jewels in. I shall give it to her."

So he did, and the queen liked the gift. That night she took off her bracelets and earrings and necklaces and put them in the pot, then put the lid on to keep them safe. But later, when she tried to take the lid off, it wouldn't budge! She tried and tried to pull it off, and then she called for the king, and he tried and tried, too.

The little pot giggled and shook until they dropped her, and then she rolled back home, singing, "My mouth is full of jewels! *Tunjur! Tunjur! Tunjur!*"

When the pot's mother saw the jewels, she said, "Oh, little pot, these jewels do not belong to you. I can see that you do not know right from wrong. Tomorrow you will take these things back to their owner and say you are sorry."

But the next morning the little pot got up early and sneaked out of the house. She rolled into the market, singing, "*Tunjur! Tunjur! Tunjur!*"

The honey seller saw the pot and said, "Surely this is the same little pot that stole my honey! I shall take it to the king and it shall get what it deserves!"

So the honey seller took the pot to the king. But when the king saw the pot, he said, "This is the pot that stole the queen's jewels! Take it out to the goat pens and fill it up with what it deserves!"

"Oh, goody!" thought the little pot. "I am going to get a reward!"

The servants took the little pot out to the goat pen. Do you know what they filled it up with? Muck and goat droppings!

The little pot rolled home, crying, "My mouth is full of muck! I don't like it! *Tunjur! Tunjur! Tunjur!*"

When the little pot got home, her mother said, "Well, little pot, I see you have found out what happens when you do wrong instead of right. I hope you have learned your lesson."

And the little pot had. That very day she went to the honey seller and the king and apologized, and took the queen back her jewels. After that the little pot always thought about right and wrong before acting and was not allowed to go to the market alone.

# Fingerplays and Songs

### 366  Going to the Market

Discuss how people around the world carry things on their heads. Then say the following rhyme. Invite a child to the front to help you act it out. Place a paper plate on the child's head and fill it with plastic food as you say the rhyme. Or get everyone in on the fun by passing out plates to each child, along with a packet of pictures of the food. Ask the children to place the plates on their heads, then add the correct food when it is said in the rhyme.

I'm going to the market, I'm going just like that.
I will buy potatoes and put them in my hat.

Repeat with tomatoes, apples, mangos, grapes, bananas, cheese, bread, and other foods as desired.

### 367 *To the Fair: A Rhyme from Hungary (adapted traditional)

Use stuffed animals, puppets, or flannelboard animals to bring this rhyme to life.

I took a penny to the fair,
And I bought a little hen there.
Then my hen said, "Cluck, cluck, cluck."
Little bitty, sweetie henny,
I will bring another penny.

I took a penny to the fair,
And I bought a little ducky there.
Then my duck said, "Quack, quack, quack."
And my hen said, "Cluck, cluck, cluck."
Little bitty, sweetie henny,
I will bring another penny.

Repeat with other animals.

### 368 To Market All Around the World (to the tune of "Twinkle, Twinkle Little Star")

To market, to market
To buy a fat pig.
Home again, home again, jiggety-jig.

Now let's speak French!

*Sur le marché* (syoor luh mar-shay), *sur le marché*
To buy me some bread.
Home again, home again, jiggety-jed.

Now let's speak Spanish!

*Al mercado* (ahl mair-CAH-doe), *al mercado*
To buy a tortilla.
Home again, home again, jiggety-jia.

Now let's speak German!

*Auf den Markt* (off den marked), *Auf den Markt*
To buy a fat sausage.
Home again, home again, jiggety-jausage.

Now let's speak Japanese!

*Shijo ni* (shee-joe nee), *shijo ni*
To buy us some rice.
Home again, home again, jiggety-jice!

To market, to market
All around the world.
Home again, home again,
Good boys and girls!

# Craft

### 369 **Native Mexican Baskets**

The Aztecs and their descendants have been making colorful baskets from palm fibers for centuries. These baskets are traditionally decorated in stripes of bright colors and are used to carry items to and from the market.

*Materials:* paper plate, stapler, crayons or markers

*Directions:*

1. Decorate both sides of the paper plate.
2. Lay the paper plate in front of you. Create four corners by pinching the edges of the plate together and stapling them.

# 39

## Spring

· · · · · · · · · · · · · · · · · · · · · · · · · · · · · · · · ·

## Books

**370** *Butterflies for Kiri* **by Cathryn Falwell. New York: Lee and Low, 2003.**

Kiri, a Japanese American girl, loves to paint and draw. But when her aunt sends her an origami book and special paper, she struggles to learn how to make an origami butterfly. At last, she succeeds in bringing all her favorite art forms together. Follow the story by teaching how to make an origami butterfly using the instructions in the book.

**371** *\*Kite Flying* **by Grace Lin. New York: Random House, 2002.**

A young girl and her family create and fly a dragon kite. The afterword describes Chinese kite-flying traditions.

**372** *How Mama Brought the Spring* **by Fran Manushkin. New York: Dutton, 2008.**

When a little girl doesn't want to leave her bed, her mother promises to tell her the story of how her grandmother brought spring to Minsk, Russia, if she gets up. The secret to spring is found in the kitchen and in the making of the special treats called *blintzes*.

**373** *The Kite Festival* **by Leyla Torres. New York: Farrar, Straus and Giroux, 2004.**

A young Colombian boy and his family travel to San Vicente for the kite festival, but the kite store is closed. They use found objects to make their own hexagonal kite, and they win a prize for the most original kite in the festival.

# Flannelboards

### 374 **Springtime Festivals**

Spring is the time to celebrate, it's my favorite time of year.
With colors and music bursting forth, we let out a happy cheer.

In India the biggest paint fight takes place during Holi.
Wear your play clothes, get your paint, and go around corners slowly.

If dancing around a May Day pole sounds fun to you,
Grab some flowers and a ribbon and put on your dancing shoes.

Around the world children say "I love you" to their mothers.
On that special day they are given cards and kisses, one after another.

Carnival is fun, it's one big party in the street.
Parades, costumes, and dancing, and lots of people to meet.

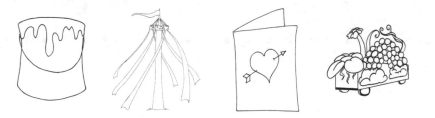

### 375 **Coyote Steals the Spring**

Adapted from Jean M. Pollock's version of the Native American tale in *Side by Side: Twelve Multicultural Puppet Plays* (Lanham, MD: Scarecrow Press, 1998).

Long ago, there was an old woman who kept the winter, spring, summer, and fall. She kept each in a leather pouch, and all the pouches hung in a line from the wall in her home. When it was time for the seasons to change, she would open the next bag. When it was fall and she decided it was time for winter, she would open the winter bag. Winter would rush out and swirl around and drive fall back to her, and she would catch it in the bag. Then winter would lie over the land, with snow and ice and rushing winds.

Once it was winter for so long that all the animals thought that old woman had forgotten about them. Rabbit's tail shivered as he searched for grass to eat. Bear yawned and yawned—he was always sleepy in the cold. And Coyote's nose was blue with cold as he went to visit his friend Bear.

Bear's cave happened to be near the old woman's tepee. They could hear her snoring inside it.

"It's been winter for a loooong time, Coyote," said Bear with a yawn. "I can't find anything to eat under all this snow!"

"I know," said Coyote thoughtfully. "But the old woman is still sleeping. I think she has forgotten all about the spring."

"If she doesn't wake up and let spring out soon, we'll all starve!" said Rabbit, shivering.

"Maybe we could take matters into our own hands," said Coyote. "Why should we wait for her to wake up? Let's let spring out ourselves!"

"How can we do it?" said Bear. "We are not quiet enough or quick enough to steal the bag without waking the old woman."

"Speak for yourself!" said Rabbit. "I am quiet *and* quick. I can do it."

"But what if she catches you?" said Bear. "You would get tired before you ran very far, and then she would get spring back right away."

"But I can run long distances!" said Coyote. "So Rabbit will steal the bag and give it to me, and I will run very far."

"But you are not strong," said Rabbit. "How will you tear open the bag to let spring out?"

"I am strong!" said Bear. "So Rabbit, you steal the bag and give it to Coyote, then Coyote will run far so that the old woman won't catch him, then I will tear open the bag and let spring out!"

They all thought about this for a while, and it seemed like a good plan. But then Bear said, "What if the old woman wakes up and says magic words to stop us?"

"I know!" said Rabbit. "I will take some honey into the tepee with me. Before I steal the bag I will smack her on the mouth with the honey. Her lips will be stuck together so she can't say magic words!"

They all agreed that this was an excellent plan. So Rabbit went to get some honey, and Bear went to a spot that he and Coyote agreed on. Then Coyote waited outside the tepee while Rabbit sneaked inside.

Rabbit crept up to the old woman and smacked the honey onto her mouth. She woke up and yelled, "Hey!" and then "Yum, honey!" She was so distracted she didn't even notice Rabbit slipping out of the tepee with the spring bag.

Rabbit tossed the bag to Coyote, who took off running. When he reached Bear, he handed over the bag. Bear ripped it open, and . . .

Flowers bloomed! Snow melted! The trees were green!

"Hooray!" cried Coyote, Bear, and Rabbit. "Spring is here!"

# Fingerplays and Songs

### 376  Cherry Blossoms

Cherry blossoms bloom high in the trees, (*reach up high*)
When the wind blows they float down past my knees. (*float fingers down*)
Their sweet smell is carried in the wind, (*sniff the air*)
And Dad tickles me with blossoms under my chin. (*tickle chin*)
I try again to reach the flowers, (*reach up high*)
But lie down to enjoy a petal shower! (*sit down*)

377 *"Haru Ga Kita"* from **Multicultural Rhythm Stick Fun** by Georgiana Stewart. Long Branch, NJ: Kimbo Educational, 1992.

When the lyrics in this Japanese song say "Flowers Grow in Spring," follow the instructions and use rhythm sticks to pretend flowers are growing.

378 **"The Maypole Song" from *Holiday Songs Around the World* by Catherine Slonecki. Freeport, NY: Educational Activities Inc., 1994.**

In the British Isles, May Day was traditionally celebrated by dancing around the maypole. Create a storytime maypole by tying lengths of crepe paper streamers to the top of a flagpole. Have the children stand in a circle around the pole and give each a streamer. For a simple pattern, stagger the children so that the inner circle is facing right and the outer circle is facing left. Then ask them to dance around the pole when the music starts.

# Craft

379 **Hawaiian Lei**

*Materials:* flower shapes cut from paper, yarn, tube pasta

*Directions:*

1. Cut yarn long enough to go over head.
2. String paper flowers and tube pasta on the yarn.
3. When complete, tie both ends together with a knot.

# 40

# Summer

• • • • • • • • • • • • • • • • • • • • • • • • • • • • • • • • • • • • • • •

## Books

**380**  *Cactus Hotel* **by Brenda Guiberson. New York: Henry Holt, 1991.**

The saguaro cactus can be found only in the Sonoran Desert of southern Arizona and northern Mexico. This story tells how the saguaro cactus brings life to the dry, hot desert, providing beauty, food, and a home for many of the desert animals and insects.

**381**  *\*¡Bravo!* **by Ginger Foglesong Guy. New York: HarperCollins, 2010.**

A brother and sister spend a summer day discovering the outdoors. This book features a simple but effective text in Spanish and English.

**382**  *At the Beach* **by Huy Voun Lee. New York: Henry Holt, 1994.**

Xiao Ming and his mother spend the day at the beach, and he learns the Chinese characters for the things they see. This book does an excellent job of showing how Chinese characters represent concepts through pictures. Explain that our alphabet represents sounds, while in Chinese writing, each symbol represents an idea. For a fun follow-up activity, copy and enlarge the symbols and illustrations from the endpapers of the book. Mix up the pictures and see if the children can match each picture to the symbol that goes with it.

**383**  *\*Hello Ocean / Hola Mar* **by Pam Muñoz Ryan. Watertown, MA: Charlesbridge, 2003.**

A little girl uses all her senses to explore the beach in this bilingual English/Spanish book.

# Flannelboard

### 384 Huckleberry Harvest

Native Americans in the Pacific Northwest have picked huckleberries for hundreds of years. These delicious berries are prized by humans and bears alike, making the huckleberry harvest an annual race between man and beast.

5 little huckleberries, not one more,
I picked 1 and then there were 4.
Along came a bear, looking for a treat,
But I ate that berry, it sure was sweet.

4 little huckleberries so beautiful to see,
I picked 1 and then there were 3.
Along came a bear, looking for a treat,
But I ate that berry, it sure was sweet.

3 little huckleberries on the bush grew,
I picked 1 and then there were 2.
Along came a bear, looking for a treat,
But I ate that berry, it sure was sweet.

2 little huckleberries hanging in the sun,
I picked 1 and then there was 1.
Along came a bear, looking for a treat,
But I ate that berry, it sure was sweet.

1 little huckleberry, oh what fun,
I picked it and then there were none.
"Please," said the bear, "I want a treat."
I gave him that berry, aren't I sweet!

# Fingerplays and Songs

### 385 Midsummer's Eve Festival

Midsummer's Eve is one of the most popular festivals in Sweden. It is a national holiday, and families and friends meet, eat special foods, and dance. The day of the celebration is also the longest day of the year (summer solstice), signifying that the year has reached the halfway point.

Midsummer's Eve is the time of year
When all Swedish people let out a cheer. (*raise hand to cheer*)
The sun shines through the day and night,
Much to the joyful children's delight. (*make a big circle in the air and smile*)

A maypole is raised to dance around,
And all the people come from the town. (*dance in place*)
There's singing and dancing and good food to eat,
Everyone thinks it is quite a treat. (*pretend to eat*)

So pick your bouquet and join in the celebration,
People in Sweden think it's quite a sensation. (*pick your bouquet*)

### 386 Summer Olympics

In ancient Greece the Olympics were tests of strength and skill.
If you were lucky enough to win, it was quite a thrill.
There are some who like to compete during a foot race,
Although only one can gain fame by finishing in first place. (*run in place*)

Careful where you sit during the discus throwing event,
Often the athlete doesn't know where the discus went. (*duck*)
Boxing was a popular sport that landed a one-two punch.
It's best to box in the morning, before you have lunch. (*pretend to box*)

Equestrian sports included races with a horse,
Climb into your chariot and let them run with force. (*gallop*)
After days of sport, whether they end in victory or defeat,
It's time to celebrate with a banquet, sit down and eat. (*sit*)

### 387 "Bahama Beach Game" from *Multicultural Bean Bag Fun* by Georgiana Stewart. Long Branch, NJ: Kimbo Educational, 2009.

Beanbags take to the beach in this catchy tune from the Bahamas.

### 388 "Put the Lime in the Coconut" from *Drew's Famous Kids Party Music*. Kenilworth, NJ: Turn Up the Music, 2000.

Dance along with this Caribbean classic and shake it up with egg shakers.

# Craft

### 389 Japanese Palace Fan

In ancient Japanese palaces, silk fans with writing and artwork were so prized that many were pre-served in albums.

*Materials:* craft stick, glue, fan shape (from template on website) cut from cardstock or posterboard, crayons or markers

*Directions:*

1. Decorate the fan as desired.
2. Glue the craft stick to the fan to make a handle.

# 41

# Transportation

. . . . . . . . . . . . . . . . . . . . . . . . . . . . . . . . . . . . .

## Books

**390** ***Rolling Along: The Story of Taylor and His Wheelchair*** **by Jamee Riggio Heelan. Atlanta: Peachtree, 2000.**

Taylor, a little boy with cerebral palsy, learns to get around in his wheelchair just as well as his twin brother. This cleverly illustrated book combines photos, collage, and illustrations with a straightforward, positively focused text.

**391** ***\*How Will We Get to the Beach? A Guessing-Game Story*** **by Brigitte Luciani. New York: NorthSouth Books, 2000.**

This wonderful storytime book was originally published in Switzerland and features a mother and baby trying to make their way to the beach. With each different method they try, however, something vital must be left behind. This is a great participatory read as the kids will need to study the illustrations to figure out which item is missing on each page.

**392** ***On the Go*** **by Ann Morris. New York: Mulberry, 1990.**

Simple text and color photos explore different types of transportation around the world. The text emphasizes the commonalities, while the photos show the variety of transportation in different cultures. A photo index identifies the origins of all the methods discussed.

**393** ***\*Wombat Walkabout*** **by Carol Diggory Shields. New York: Dutton, 2009.**

Six little wombats go on a walkabout in the Australian outback, but they don't know that a dingo is eyeing them for his lunch. This bouncy rhyming tale, accompanied by large, appealing, storytime-ready illustrations, counts down the little wombats as the nasty dingo catches them, then relates how the last two wombats trick the dingo and free their friends.

# Flannelboards

### 394  Sean's Transportation

Many Spanish words sound a lot like words in English. Share the following sentences and see if the children can guess what the Spanish words mean, then practice saying the Spanish words together as a group.

> What vehicle is it?: *¿Qué es el vehículo?* (keh ess el veh-EE-coo-lo)
> bus: *autobús* (aooh-toe-BOOSS)
> airplane: *avión* (ah-VEEON)
> car: *coche* (KOH-cheh)
> train: *tren* (trehn)
> bicycle: *bicicleta* (bee-see-CLEH-tah)

Some days Sean takes an *autobús*. *¿Qué es el vehículo?* (bus)
Sean likes to take an *avión* on vacation. *¿Qué es el vehículo?* (airplane)
Sometimes Sean has to drive his dogs around in a *coche*. *¿Qué es el vehículo?* (car)
Sean's favorite thing to ride on is a *tren*. *¿Qué es el vehículo?* (train)
When Sean's home, he rides his *bicicleta* to his friend's house. *¿Qué es el vehículo?* (bike)

### 395  How Do We Get Around?

Venice is a watery city, where instead of cars they use boats.
To get to work each day, climb in a gondola and down the canal we'll float.

Sweden is a land of wintry snow and ice.
If you need to go to town, snowshoes and skis are very nice.

Navigating the crowded streets of India requires strength and skill.
When riding in a rickshaw, you have to help the driver push uphill.

The Middle East is a land full of vast deserts and heat.
If you need a ride to an oasis, a camel can't be beat.

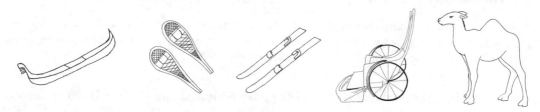

# Fingerplays and Songs

### 396 My Boat Is Going: A Rhyme from Lebanon (adapted traditional)

Have the children hold hands in a circle. As the boat in the rhyme is going out to sea, everyone should back up, making the circle as wide as possible. When the boat comes back, everyone rushes in to the middle. Repeat, each time inviting a different child to say what he or she would want the boat to carry.

My boat is going, going away to sea.
Now my boat is coming back!
My boat is carrying sugar and tea.

### 397 *"Walking Song (Switzerland)" from *Children's Folk Dances* by Georgiana Stewart. Long Branch, NJ: Kimbo Educational, 1998.

Using a traditional Swiss folk melody, this movement song encourages children to imagine walking through the Alps.

### 398 "London Drive" from *Multicultural Bean Bag Fun* by Georgiana Stewart. Long Branch, NJ: Kimbo Educational, 2009.

Beanbags become cars in this silly song. Follow the directions in the lyrics as the song takes kids on a trip through London, England.

### 399 "The World Is Big, the World Is Small" from *Multicultural Children's Songs* by Ella Jenkins. Washington, DC: Smithsonian Folkways, 1995.

Act out the words of this song about the many ways to travel.

# Craft

### 400 *ASL "Handy" Boat

This simple craft demonstrates the sign BOAT.

*Materials:* boat piece, flag, and two handshapes cut from construction paper (from template on website); one 6-by-1-inch strip of construction paper for crosspiece; craft stick; glue

*Directions:*

1. Fold the boat piece in half.
2. Glue the hands to the outside of the boat so that the thumbs are at the top and the fingers of both hands are pointing the same way.
3. Fold the crosspiece down 1 inch from each end. Glue the folded ends to the inside of the boat, so that the crosspiece keeps the boat open.
4. Glue the craft stick to the inside of the boat to form the mast.
5. Glue the flag to the top of the craft stick.
6. Decorate as desired.

# 42

# Under the Sea

## Books

**401** ***Nanook and Pryce*** **by Ned Crowley. New York: HarperCollins, 2009.**

Two Inuit boys, Nanook and Pryce, along with their dog, Yukon, start their day ice fishing in the icy arctic. Soon they are adrift in the ocean, traveling around the world and encountering many sea creatures. Using a map, point out Nanook and Pryce's route and tell what countries they passed.

**402** ***The Fisherman and the Turtle*** **by Eric A. Kimmel. Tarrytown, NY: Marshall Cavendish, 2008.**

This retelling of "The Fisherman and His Wife" is set in the Aztec empire of Mexico and incorporates elements from "The Crown of Sang Nila Utama," a folktale from Singapore. A poor fisherman meets a wish-granting sea turtle and finds that nothing is enough for his greedy wife.

**403** ***Surf War!*** **by Margaret Read MacDonald. Atlanta: August House, 2009.**

Whale and Sandpiper's argument over who owns the sea leads to all-out war as they call on their various relatives for support. The message in this folktale from the Marshall Islands is a simple but profound one: our world is so interconnected that when we hurt others, we also hurt ourselves. After reading the story, show the Marshall Islands on a map. Ask the children why they think it would be especially important to this culture for everyone to share the sea.

**404** ***The Day the Ocean Came to Visit*** **by Diane Wolkstein. San Diego, CA: Harcourt, 2001.**

This Nigerian folktale explains why the sun and the moon live in the sky. A long time ago, when they lived on Earth, Sun and Moon invited their friend Ocean to visit. She was so huge that she flooded their house, so they had no choice but to jump up into the sky.

# Flannelboard

## 405 The Gossiping Clams: A Native American Legend

Adapted from "The Gossiping Clams (Suquamish)" in *Apples from Heaven: Multicultural Folk Tales about Stories and Storytellers* by Naomi Baltuck (North Haven, CT: Shoe String Press, 1995).

A long time ago, all the animals could talk. The clams talked most of all. Do you know why? It was because they had such *big* mouths. See how their mouths were as big as their whole bodies?

The clams lived on the dry sand at the beach, and they loved to tell stories. Sometimes their stories were true. Sometimes they weren't.

One day Eagle came to the beach and caught a fish. While he was eating it, the clams said, "Raven says he is a much better hunter than you are!"

Eagle's feathers bristled. "He is not!" he said indignantly. "I actually hunt for my food. All Raven does is pick at other animals' leftovers."

Eagle flew away in a huff. The clams giggled. Raven hadn't really said that—they just liked to make up stories. And even if Raven had said it, it wasn't very nice of the clams to repeat it and make Eagle feel bad.

Later that day, Otter came to play in the water. "Oh," the clams said, "you aren't really lazy, like Beaver says. You just like to have fun."

Otter stared at the clams. Her feelings were hurt. "Lazy? Me?"

"Well," said the clams, "you know how Beaver is. He thinks everyone should work as hard as he does."

"But I thought Beaver was my friend," said Otter. She didn't feel like playing anymore. She sadly left the water.

The clams did this again and again, until all the animals were angry at each other or had their feelings hurt. Finally Raven got so sick of the clams' gossiping that he called a council meeting.

"We must do something about the clams and their mean stories!" said Raven. "Beaver, you are a hard worker. We know that you will work on this problem until you have found a solution. Could you help us?"

"Yes," said Beaver, and he thought and thought.

Finally he gathered up all the clams and carried them to the edge of the water.

"Wait! Stop! What are you doing?" squeaked the clams.

"You'll see," said Beaver. Beaver waited until the tide went out, and quickly buried each clam in the wet sand! The clams were angry! When Otter and Raven and the other animals came by, the clams opened their mouths to tattle on Beaver, and guess what happened? Their mouths filled up with wet sand! They sputtered and spit out the water. Each time they tried to open their mouths, the same thing happened.

Even today when you walk along the beach, you might see water spurting up from the sand. That's the clams spitting out the water and sand they swallowed when they opened their mouths to try to gossip!

# Fingerplays and Songs

### 406 *Tong, Tong, Tong, Tong*: A Traditional Rhyme from the Philippines

*Tong, tong, tong, tong, pakitong-kitong.* (*scuttle sideways*)
Crabs in the sea! (*mime pincers*)
So big and tasty, (*stretch arms wide*)
Tough to catch, (*mime catching*)
Because they *bite*! (*clap hands*)
*Tong, tong, tong, tong, pakitong-kitong.* (*scuttle sideways*)

### 407 *A la Víbora de la Mar* / Sea Serpent

This Mexican game is played like "London Bridge": the children make two lines facing one another and hold hands up high to make a bridge. The children on the end go under the bridge. The last two children in line drop their hands down and capture the last child on the last line.

Sea serpent, sea serpent,
Come on through.
Here's a pathway just for you.
Those in front, run through fast.
The gates will close upon the last.
Last! Last! Last!

*A la víbora, víbora* (ah la VEE-bo-rah)
*de la mar, de la mar* (deh la mahr)
*por aquí pueden pasar.* (pore ah-KEE PWEH-den pah-sar)
*Los de adelante corren mucho* (los deh ah-deh-LAHN-teh CO-ren MOO-cho)
*y los de atrás se quedarán* (ee los deh ah-TRAHS seh keh-dar-AN)
*tras, tras, tras, tras.* (trahs)

### 408 Here Is the Sea: An Australian Hand Rhyme (adapted traditional)

Here is the sea, (*hold palms together in front of body*)
The wavy sea, (*wiggle palms back and forth*)
Here is a boat, (*open palms to make boat*)
And here is me! (*sit bent index and middle fingers of right hand in left palm*)
All the fishes down below, (*keep left palm in place and move right hand below*)
Wiggle their tails (*wiggle right hand to represent fish*)
And away they go!

### 409 "Under the Sea" from *The Little Mermaid* by Alan Menken. Burbank, CA: Walt Disney Records, 2006.

Enjoy this calypso-style tune as you dance around with drums and rhythm sticks. Calypso is a style of Afro-Caribbean music that originated in Trinidad and Tobago.

# Craft

### 410 Fish Tangram

A tangram is a Chinese puzzle that is made of seven shapes. You can arrange the shapes to make different patterns and pictures.

*Materials:* tangram template (from website), construction paper, scissors, crayons, glue

*Directions:*

1. Cut the seven shapes out of the tangram template.
2. Experiment with the shapes by putting them together in different ways to create a fish.
3. When you have the shapes the way you want them, glue them down on a piece of construction paper.
4. Decorate as desired.

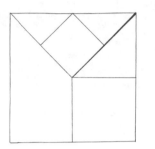

# 43

# Weather

## Books

**411** ***Bringing the Rain to Kapiti Plain*** **by Verna Aardema. New York: Dial, 1981.**

In this African folktale a herdsman named Ki-pat needs rain for the grass to grow so his cows do not die. Ki-pat makes a bow and arrow and shoots the arrow into the black rain cloud, bringing rain to Kapiti Plain.

**412** ***The Black Book of Colors*** **by Menena Cottin and Rosana Faria, translated by Elisa Amado. Toronto, ON: Groundwood Books, 2006.**

This unique book presents colors from the perspective of a blind boy, each with a correlation to a texture in the natural world. The text appears in white on completely black pages (and in Braille), with raised black-on-black illustrations meant to be experienced by touch.

**413** ***Boat Ride with Lillian Two Blossom*** **by Patricia Polacco. New York: Philomel, 1988.**

Will is trying to fish, but his younger sister Mabel keeps scaring away the fish with noisy questions like "What makes it rain?" and "Where does the wind come from?" Out from the bushes comes Lillian Two Blossom, an elderly Native American woman, who takes them on a magical boat ride to find the answers.

**414** ***Rain Player*** **by David Wisniewski. New York: Clarion, 1991.**

In this Mayan tale, a boy named Pik challenges Chac, the god of rain, to a game of *pok-a-tok*—a cross between soccer and basketball—in order to avert a foretold drought that would devastate his people. Pik's father gives him three talismans to help in the play-off against the fierce sky god, and with their aid the boy is victorious.

# Flannelboards

### 415  *The Rat: A Folktale from China

This story can also be told as a dramatic retelling, with child volunteers taking the parts and acting it out. To tell this story as a prop story, you will need:

- a pair of rat ears on a headband
- a brown or black blanket (have the child playing the rock crouch down and drape the blanket over him or her)
- a sun mask on a stick
- a cloud (for a simple cloud costume, cut a cloud shape out of white posterboard or cotton batting and tie a string to it so that the child can wear it around his or her neck)
- a streamer to represent the wind

Once upon a time, there was a little rat. He lived under a rock in the mountains, and each day he would gnaw at it, to make his burrow larger. The sun shone down on him, and he got so hot that one day he said, "Ai! The sun is surely the most powerful thing in the world! I wish I could be the sun!"

And just like that, he became the sun! He shone down on the people below, making them sweat, and he said, "Yes, I am the most powerful thing in the world!" But then a strange thing happened. Something drifted in front of him, blocking his rays. It was a cloud! He said, "Ai! What's this? The cloud is blocking my rays! Then the cloud is surely the most powerful thing in the world! I wish I could be the cloud!"

And just like that, he became the cloud! He moved across the sky, raining here, snowing there, and said, "Surely I am the most powerful thing in the world!"

But then a strange thing happened. He felt himself being blown around, and he couldn't stop it! "What's this?" he cried. "The wind is blowing me hither and thither! The wind is surely the most powerful thing in the world! I wish I could be the wind!"

And just like that, he became the wind! He blew all around, over rivers and across the grass, enjoying how he could make the leaves swirl up. But then a strange thing happened. He blew up against a rock, and it wouldn't move! "Ai! The rock is surely the most powerful thing in the world! I wish I could be the rock!"

And just like that, he became the rock! He sat there on the mountainside, strong and unmovable, and said to himself, "Surely, I, the rock, am now the most powerful thing in the world!"

But then a strange thing happened. He felt something tickling him, and he looked down to find a little rat gnawing at him, pieces of him falling away as the rat made his burrow larger. "What's this?" he said. "The rat is more powerful than me! Why then surely the rat is the most powerful thing in the world! I wish to be a rat again!"

And just like that, he became a rat again. And from then on he lived content in the shadow of the rock, knowing that he was the most powerful thing in the world.

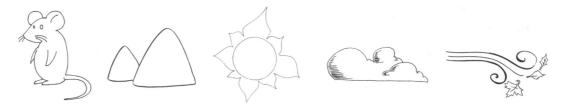

### 416  Grandmother Spider Brings the Light: A Native American Legend

In the beginning there was nothing but darkness. The animals couldn't see anything, and they kept bumping into each other and stepping on the tails of their friends. Finally they called a great council meeting and tried to decide what to do.

"We need light!" they all yelled.

"But how do we get it?" others questioned.

Rabbit made a suggestion. "When there is a thunderstorm, sometimes there is a crack in the sky and the light shines through. If someone were to go to the crack in the sky, he can bring back some light."

But who would be brave enough to get the light?

"I'll go," said Buzzard. "I am big and strong with long wings."

So off Buzzard flew toward the crack in the sky. When he got there, he broke off a piece of lightning and tucked it onto his head, where all of his thick, soft feathers were.

Buzzard didn't know that lightning was made of fire, but he soon learned! As he started flying, the lightning burned through his feathers and burned his head! "*Ouch!*" he cried.

The light had burned out, and he was bald!

Again, there was darkness, and the animals began asking if anyone would be brave enough to try again. Finally Possum approached. "I will go, I will get the light! I am smarter than Buzzard." So off Possum went to the crack in the sky. She broke off a piece of lightning and wondered where she should hold it. "I know, I'll put it in my nice bushy tail." As she started walking back to the other animals she screamed, "*Ouch!*" The lightning had burnt through her tail and now her tail was naked!

Again, there was darkness, and the animals began asking if anyone would be brave enough to try again.

"I will go," said a tiny voice.

The animals saw that it was Grandmother Spider who had offered, and they began laughing.

"You're too small. And you're too old. You'll get lost. You can't go!"

"I may be little and I may be old, but I think I deserve a chance," said Grandmother Spider.

The animals agreed, and Grandmother Spider started walking toward the crack in the sky. She knew she might forget her way back, so she spun a web all the way from where the animals were waiting to the light. When she got the light, she remembered what had happened to Possum and Buzzard. She scooped up some cool, wet mud and placed the light into the mud so that she wouldn't burn herself. By the time she returned to the animals, the mud was a dry, hard, glowing ball, so she threw it into the sky and there was light.

Ever since that time, Buzzard has been bald, Possum has had a naked tail, and Spider's web has been shaped like the rays of the sun.

# Fingerplays and Songs

### 417 *Pòtòpótò*: A Yoruba Riddle

*Pòtòpótò* is a word in the Yoruba language, which is spoken in parts of Nigeria and other African countries. Share this rhyme with the children and ask if they can guess what a *pòtòpótò* is.

A *pòtòpótò* can be many shapes,
Though usually they're round.
You see a *pòtòpótò*
After rain, there on the ground.

Look into a *pòtòpótò*,
You'll see your face with each eyelash.
If you jump in a *pòtòpótò*,
You will make a splash!

Can you guess the riddle now,
Or are you in a muddle?
*Pòtòpótò* is the Yoruba word
That means a . . . (puddle)!

### 418 **Today's Weather** (to the tune of "She'll Be Coming 'Round the Mountain")

Before singing this song, introduce the children to these concepts in Italian:

> sun: *il sole* (eel SOH-lay)
> rain: *la pioggia* (la pee-OH-ja)
> wind: *il vento* (eel VEN-toh)

*Il sole* will surely shine a lot today, oh *il sole* will surely shine a lot today,
We'll play around and have some fun, 'cause that's what we do in *il sole*.
*Il sole* will surely shine a lot today.

*La pioggia* will surely fall a lot today, oh *la pioggia* will surely fall a lot today,
And we know the sticky mud'll be right inside the puddle.
*La pioggia* will surely fall a lot today.

*Il vento* will surely blow a lot today, oh *il vento* will surely blow a lot today,
So hold onto your hat, as it blows away like that.
*Il vento* will surely blow a lot today.

**419** ***Spider Song: A Song in ASL and English** (adapted traditional)

The medium-sized SPIDER went up the waterspout.

Down came the RAIN and washed the SPIDER out.

Out came the SUN and DRIED up all the rain,

And the medium-sized SPIDER went up the spout again.

But right next door lived . . . the *great big* SPIDER!

Repeat song, singing more loudly and signing with larger movements.

And right next door to him lived . . . the *teeny tiny* SPIDER!

Repeat song, singing in a tiny voice and signing with tiny movements.

# Craft

### 420 **Chinese Dancing Ribbon**

The Ribbon Dance is a two-thousand-year-old folk dance. Dancers use long ribbons attached to sticks to represent clouds, and the dance is supposed to bring rain and plentiful crops.

*Materials:* two 30-inch pieces of ribbon, craft stick

*Directions:*

1. Tie ribbons securely to one end of the craft stick.
2. Play some Chinese music and invite the children to perform their own ribbon dance, swaying the ribbons up, down, in waves, and all around.

# 44
# Winter

## Books

**421** ***The Three Snow Bears*** **by Jan Brett. New York: Putnam, 2007.**

This snowy version of "Goldilocks and the Three Bears" features Aloo-ki, an Inuit girl who explores the igloo of three polar bears.

**422** ***The Ant and the Grasshopper*** **by Amy Lowry Poole. New York: Holiday House, 2000.**

This lovely retelling of the classic Aesop fable is set in the Emperor's summer palace in China, and the art was created using traditional Chinese materials. While the ants busily prepare for the coming winter, the grasshopper sings, plays music, and frolics in the gardens. When winter comes, he wishes he had heeded the ants' advice.

**423** ***The Sun's Daughter*** **by Pat Sherman. New York: Clarion, 2005.**

Based on the Iroquois legend of the Corn Maiden, this pourquoi tale explains why winter exists—the sun mourns when her daughter Maize is taken from her each year, and her daughter can only return to her when the "trees weep."

**424** ***The Snow*** **by Huy Voun Lee. New York: Henry Holt, 1995.**

Xiao Ming and his mother go for a walk in the snow and practice writing in Chinese. The text introduces Chinese characters for snow-related words. Explain that our alphabet represents sounds, while in Chinese writing, each symbol represents an idea. For a fun follow-up activity, copy and enlarge the symbols and illustrations from the endpapers of the book. Mix up the pictures and see if the children can match each picture to the symbol that goes with it.

# Flannelboard

### 425 *The Snow Child: A Folktale from Russia

Once upon a time, there was an old man and old woman who were very sad because they didn't have any children. "If only I had a child to walk with me on snowy afternoons," said the old man. "If only I had a child to sing to," said the old woman. So one wintry day, the old man and the old woman decided to build a child out of snow. They rolled together snowballs and made a body, arms, legs, and even hair for their little snow child. The old woman dressed the snow child in a little blue dress she had made herself. Then she leaned over and kissed the snow child.

All at once, the snow child came to life! "Mama! Papa!" she cried, and hugged the old man and woman with her chilly arms. The old man and the old woman were overjoyed! They spent the whole day playing with their snow child. The old man took the snow child for long walks in the snow, and the old woman sang songs to her. That night, they tried to take her inside with them, but she began to melt by the fire. So they made a little bed for her in the garden, and she slept soundly all night under the wintry stars.

That winter passed very happily for the old man and the old woman and their snow child. The snow child made friends with the village children and spent happy hours roaming through the snowy forest and meeting all the little birds.

But then, one day, the snow began to melt, and the sun shone a little brighter. Spring birds began to return from the south, and the snow child grew sad. By the time the last snow had melted away, the snow child would not do anything but sulk in her bed all day long.

"What shall we do?" said the old man.

"Our snow child needs the snow," said the old woman sadly. "We must let her go where she can be happy."

So they went out to the garden and told the snow child, "We know that you are unhappy to be without the snow. We are your parents and will always love you. Go to where the snowy winds blow, but come back to us when those winds blow here."

The snow child kissed her parents with cold, cold lips and said, "Thank you, Mama and Papa! I will always love you, and I will always come to you when the cold winds blow."

And so the snow child blew away to the north, but every autumn when the winds blow cold, she keeps her promise and returns to her parents.

# Fingerplays and Songs

### 426  *La Neige Tombe* / Snow Is Falling: A Rhyme from Canada in French and English (adapted traditional)

*La neige tombe* (la NEZH tohmb), snow is falling on my nose!
Uh-oh! My nose froze!
I rub, rub, rub my nose
To warm it up!
I rub, rub, rub my nose
To warm it up!

*La neige tombe*, snow is falling on my hands!
Uh-oh! Cold, frozen hands!
I clap, clap, clap, my hands
To warm them up!
I clap, clap, clap, my hands
To warm them up!

### 427  Russian Troika (to the tune of "Dreidel")

As you sing the song, invite the children to trot in a circle, pretending to hold their horses' reins. Invite the children to suggest different ways the sled can move, such as fast, slow, over a bumpy road, and so on. Repeat the song, moving the troika a different way each time.

I have a little troika my horses pull along,
And when we go a-riding, we sing this little song.
Oh troika, troika, troika, you pull us in the snow,
Oh troika, troika, troika, a-sledding you will go.

### 428  *The Sign for Snow: A Rhyme in ASL and English

When the weather is cold, and the icy wind blows,
And you feel a shiver right down to your toes,
Wiggle your fingers from the sky to the ground.
That's the sign for SNOW you have found!

### 429 *Snowshoes, Snowshoes

Snowshoes were made for hundreds of years by Native American tribes who live in snowy areas. Each tribe had its own design tailored to the type of snow in which its members needed to move. Discuss what snowshoes are and invite the children to perform the following rhyme as if wearing snowshoes.

Snowshoes, snowshoes, step so high.
Snowshoes, snowshoes, to the sky.
Snowshoes, snowshoes, turn around.
Snowshoes, snowshoes, touch the ground.
Snowshoes, snowshoes, make a ball of snow.
Snowshoes, snowshoes, give it a throw!

# Craft

### 430 Winter Solstice Wreath

Wreaths are associated with winter customs in many different countries and are typically made with evergreens to symbolize strength, as evergreens last even through the harshest winters. The circular shape of the wreath represents the continuity of the seasons.

*Materials:* a paper plate, an assortment of pine cones, twigs, greens, glue, yarn or ribbon bows, glitter

*Directions:*

1. Cut the center out of a paper plate.
2. Glue pine cones and other natural materials around the paper plate edge.
3. Decorate as desired with glitter, bows made from ribbon or yarn, and so on.
4. The wreath can either be hung on the wall or laid on a table with a candle placed in the center to light the winter nights.

# APPENDIX A

# Culture Notes and Index of Entries by Culture

Starred items are especially appropriate to use with toddlers.

**AFRICA** is a continent containing fifty-three individual countries.

**Benin** is located on the coast of Africa. Family is very important in Benin, and children are expected to be obedient and show respect for their elders.

**Botswana** is a landlocked country in southern Africa. The tribe is an important unit in Botswana, as it provides both emotional and financial security.

**The Democratic Republic of the Congo** is located in Africa and was first settled by the Pygmies. Most people in Congo live in the southwestern portion of the country, leaving the tropical jungle in the north uninhabited.

*Ghana* is located in western Africa. Ghanaian society is hierarchical, with elders occupying the most respected place.

> *Pretty Salma: A Little Red Riding Hood Story from Africa* by Niki Daly (Fairy Tales)

*Kenya* is home to an extremely diverse culture made up of forty different ethnic groups. The family is the primary social unit, and the concept of *harambee* (from a Bantu word meaning "to pull together") defines the people's approach to life.

> *For You Are a Kenyan Child* by Kelly Cunnane (My Neighborhood)
>
> *Mama Panya's Pancakes* by Mary and Rich Chamberlin (Shopping)
>
> *My Library Flannelboard (Books and Libraries)
>
> My School (School Days)

*Liberia* was founded and colonized by freed American black slaves in the 1820s. Liberia is known for its decorative masks and wood carvings.

> *Koi and the Kola Nuts* by Verna Aardema (Nature)

*Malawi* is located in southeastern Africa. People in Malawi typically live with their extended families in huts, grouped together in villages.

> *Galimoto* by Karen Lynn Williams (Playtime)

*Morocco* is located in northern Africa. Ninety-nine percent of Moroccans are Muslim. Moroccan culture values family, the subordination of the individual to the group, and the concept of personal honor.

> *My Father's Shop* by Satomi Ichikawa (Shopping)

*Nigeria* is home to a culture in which the most senior person in the group is greeted and served first and has the responsibility to make decisions for the group.

> *The Day the Ocean Came to Visit* by Diane Wolkstein (Under the Sea)
>
> *Pòtòpótò: A Yoruba Riddle* (Weather)

*South Africa's* culture centers on the family and includes both the nuclear and extended family.

> *Abiyoyo* by Pete Seeger (Big and Little)
>
> *Happy Birthday, Jamela!* by Niki Daly (Shoes)
>
> *Jamela's Dress* by Niki Daly (Clothes)
>
> *One Child, One Seed: A South African Counting Book* by Kathryn Cave (Fall)
>
> *A South African Night* by Rachel Isadora (Bedtime)

*Swahili* is an official language of Tanzania, Kenya, Uganda, and the Democratic Republic of the Congo and is spoken throughout much of East Africa.

> "One Two Three" (Counting)
>
> *The World Turns Round and Round* by Nicki Weiss (Family)

*Uganda's* culture values music, with each tribe having its own music and dances to celebrate occasions.

> *Beatrice's Goat* by Page McBrier (Community Helpers)

*Zambia* is located in southern Africa. Zambia's culture mixes indigenous Bantu elements with European influences.

> Dress Up (Clothes)

*Zanzibar* is part of the United Republic of Tanzania, in east Africa. It consists of many islands off the coast of Tanzania. Its culture values hospitality, family, and honor.

> The Hare and the Lion Flannelboard or Prop Story (Houses and Homes)

*Zimbabwe* is located in the southern region of Africa. It is known for its art, particularly its Shona soapstone sculptures and wood carvings.

> *Where Are You Going, Manyoni?* by Catherine Stock (School Days)

The **Zulu** people are the largest ethnic group in South Africa. Over ten million people speak the Zulu language.

> *Can You Count Ten Toes? Count to 10 in 10 Different Languages* by Lezlie Evans (Counting)
>
> "Here Come Our Mothers" (Parents)

**See also** Middle East (Egypt), North America (African American)

African American. *See* North America

American Sign Language. *See* Deaf Culture

American Southwest. *See* North America

Appalachia. *See* North America

# ASIA is the largest continent and has over forty countries, as well as thousands of islands.

> *Tiger Tiger* by Dee Lillegard (Jungle Animals)

**Bangladesh** was formed in 1971 when it officially separated from what is now Pakistan. Bangladeshi society is hierarchical, with most decisions made by the senior male in each family.

> *Yasmin's Hammer* by Ann Malaspina (School Days)

**Bhutan** is surrounded by the Himalayan Mountains. Bhutanese society is centered on the practice of Buddhism, and prayer flags are a common sight on hillsides and rooftops.

> Four Friends Flannelboard or Prop Story (Friends)

**Cambodia** is located in Southeast Asia. Cambodia's culture is heavily influenced by India.

> My School (School Days)

**China** is one of the oldest nations in the world at over two thousand years old. Chinese culture values connections and responsibility to the group over individual freedom.

> *1, 2, 3, Go!* by Huy Voun Lee (Playtime)
>
> *The Ant and the Grasshopper* by Amy Lowry Poole (Winter)
>
> *At the Beach* by Huy Voun Lee (Summer)
>
> *Bringing in the New Year* by Grace Lin (Holidays and Celebrations)
>
> Chinese Dancing Ribbon Craft (Weather)
>
> Chinese Paper Bowl Hat Craft (Hats)
>
> Chopstick Song (Food)
>
> *The Cow (Farm Fun)
>
> *The Empty Pot* by Demi (Gardens and Growing)
>
> *Five Chinese Dragons (Holidays and Celebrations)
>
> Fish Tangram Craft (Under the Sea)
>
> *Grandfather Tang's Story: A Tale Told with Tangrams* Flannelboard (book by Ann Tompert; Forest Animals)
>
> *In the Leaves* by Huy Voun Lee (Fall)
>
> *Kite Flying* by Grace Lin (Spring)
>
> *Little Mouse (Big and Little)
>
> "The Little Rooster and the Heavenly Dragon" Flannelboard (Fairy Tales)
>
> *One Is a Drummer* by Roseanne Thong (Counting)
>
> *Rabbit's Gift* by George Shannon (Forest Animals)
>
> *The Rat Flannelboard or Prop Story (Weather)
>
> The Seven Chinese Brothers Flannelboard (Brothers and Sisters)
>
> *The Snow* by Huy Voun Lee (Winter)
>
> *Thanking the Moon: Celebrating the Mid-Autumn Moon Festival* by Grace Lin (Fall)
>
> *Three Pandas* by Jan Wahl (Brothers and Sisters)
>
> *See also* North America (Chinese American)

**Chinese** includes many different dialects within its language family, and most are so different that speakers of different dialects cannot understand one another.

*Can You Count Ten Toes? Count to 10 in 10 Different Languages* by Lezlie Evans (Counting)

Everybody's Library: A Guessing Game (Books and Libraries)

Hands (Hands)

Head and Shoulders, Baby (Counting)

Hello (Friends)

*In the Leaves* by Huy Voun Lee (Fall)

The Old Woman Who Lived in the Shoe (Shoes)

"One Two Three" (Counting)

**Hindi** is the primary official language of India.

*Can You Count Ten Toes? Count to 10 in 10 Different Languages* by Lezlie Evans (Counting)

Parents Around the World (Parents)

\*_The World Turns Round and Round_ by Nicki Weiss (Family)

**India** extends from the Himalayan Mountains to the Indian Ocean. Hinduism has a strong influence on Indian life, with hierarchies and family relationships defining the place of the individual in society.

*Andar, Bahar* (Playtime)

*"Balloon Song" (Playtime)

*The Happiest Tree: A Yoga Story* by Uma Krishnaswami (My Body)

Hello Hands (Hands)

How Do We Get Around? (Transportation)

*Little Bird (Birds)

*Mama's Saris* by Pooja Makhijani (Clothes)

Mehndi Hands Craft (Hands)

My School (School Days)

Parent's Day Card Craft (Parents)

Rakhi Celebration Bracelets Craft (Brothers and Sisters)

*Seven Blind Mice* by Ed Young (Jungle Animals)

Springtime Festivals Flannelboard (Spring)

\*_What Should I Make?_ by Nandini Nayer (Food)

**Japan** is made up of many islands off the coasts of Korea and China in the Pacific Ocean. Japanese culture values harmony and cooperation, as well as the concept of "face," or personal honor.

Cherry Blossoms (Spring)

Chopstick Song (Food)

*Close Hands, Open Hands (Hands)

Dress Up (Clothes)

*"Haru Ga Kita"* (Spring)

*Japan ABCs* by Sarah Heiman (ABC Time)

Japanese Palace Fan Craft (Summer)

*Lissy's Friends* by Grace Lin (Friends)

*One Leaf Rides the Wind: Counting in a Japanese Garden* by Celeste Davidson Mannis (Gardens and Growing)

Origami Cat Craft (Cats and Dogs)

Origami Dog Craft (Cats and Dogs)

**Japanese** is spoken by over 130 million people in Japan and emigrant communities around the world.

**Korea** is divided into two countries, North Korea and South Korea, with very different living conditions, economies, and governments. Korean culture generally values responsibility to the family and *kibun*, which loosely translates as "personal honor" or "pride."

**Korean** is spoken by 78 million people worldwide and is the official language of both North and South Korea.

**Mongolia** is located in eastern and central Asia. Its culture is heavily influenced by the Mongol nomadic tradition.

**Myanmar**, formerly known as Burma, is part of Asia and gained its independence from India in 1948. Since 1989 the military authorities have promoted the name Myanmar as the official name for the state.

**Pakistan** is located in Asia and was created when India was given its independence. Pakistani families tend to be quite large.

**The Philippines** consists of over seven thousand islands in the Pacific Ocean. Family relationships are central to culture and society, with extended families living in the same community and offering support to each other.

*Singapore* is made up of sixty-three islands, and its culture combines Malay, Chinese, Indian, and European influences.

> *The Fisherman and the Turtle* by Eric A. Kimmel (Under the Sea)

*Sri Lanka* is located in the Indian Ocean. Honor and personal integrity are very important to Sri Lankans.

> How the Baby Birds Learned to Fly Flannelboard (Birds)

*Tagalog*, also known as Filipino, is the national language of the Philippines.

> *Can You Count Ten Toes? Count to 10 in 10 Different Languages* by Lezlie Evans (Counting)

*Thailand* is located in Southeast Asia and was formerly known as Siam. Thais place great emphasis on politeness, respect, and self-control.

> *The Girl Who Wore Too Much* Flannelboard or Prop Story (book by Margaret Read MacDonald; Clothes)
>
> Hello Hands (Hands)
>
> *Hush! A Thai Lullaby* by Minfong Ho (Bedtime)
>
> *My Library Flannelboard (Books and Libraries)

*Tibet* is located north of the Himalayan Mountain region. Because it has the highest elevation on Earth, averaging sixteen thousand feet, it is known as "The Roof of the World." Buddhism exerts a strong influence on Tibetan culture.

> *All the Way to Lhasa: A Tale from Tibet* by Barbara Helen Berger (Fast and Slow)
>
> Himalayan Sherpa (Community Helpers)

*Vietnam's* culture revolves around the family, and it is not unusual for several generations to live together in one house.

> *Why Ducks Sleep on One Leg* by Sherry Garland (Farm Fun)

*Vietnamese* is the national language of Vietnam and is also spoken by large numbers of people in twenty-two other countries around the world.

> "One Two Three" (Counting)
>
> *The World Turns Round and Round* by Nicki Weiss (Family)

*See also* Europe (Russia); Middle East (Turkey)

**AUSTRALIA** is a continent and country surrounded by the Indian Ocean and Pacific Ocean. The Aboriginal people were the first people of Australia. Because of its relatively small population, Australian culture emphasizes getting along with others.

> *The Biggest Frog in Australia* by Susan L. Roth (Frogs)
>
> Here Is the Sea (Under the Sea)
>
> *Kookaburra Flannelboard (Birds)
>
> *My Library Flannelboard (Books and Libraries)
>
> My School (School Days)
>
> *Snap!* by Marcia Vaughan (Playtime)
>
> *Wombat Walkabout* by Carol Diggory Shields (Transportation)

Bahamas. *See* Caribbean

Bangladesh. *See* Asia

Belgium. *See* Europe

Benin. *See* Africa

Bhutan. *See* Asia

Botswana. *See* Africa

**THE CARIBBEAN** includes hundreds of tropical islands across the Caribbean Sea. Many people who live on these islands are descendants of slaves from Africa, the Middle East, the Far East, and India. This blending of cultures has mixed traditions and formed new languages called creoles.

**The Bahamas** are a group of over seven hundred islands. Bahamian culture is known for being friendly and informal and for valuing humor.

**Cuba** is an island off the coast of Florida. The culture of Cuba is a mixture of European, African, and North American influences.

**Haiti** is located on the island of Hispaniola. Its culture is a mix of West African and French influences.

**Jamaica** is located south of Cuba. Jamaican culture tends to distrust authority and place more value on relationships with family and close friends.

**Puerto Rico** is a territory of the United States of America. Its culture is a mix of Native Indian, Spanish, African, and North American influences.

**Trinidad and Tobago** are islands located in the Caribbean. These islands are known for their steel drum and calypso music.

**CENTRAL AMERICA** is a narrow strip of land connecting North and South America.

**Nicaragua** is known for its friendly, hospitable culture.

**Panama** is the southernmost country in Central America. Eighty-five percent of its people are Roman Catholic.

Chile. *See* South America

China. *See* Asia

Chinese (language). *See* Asia

Chinese American. *See* North America

Colombia. *See* South America

Congo. *See* Africa (The Democratic Republic of the Congo)

Cuba. *See* Caribbean

Czech Republic. *See* Europe

**DEAF CULTURE** describes the beliefs, behaviors, and values of the core deaf community in the United States and Canada. Deaf Culture values access to communication, collaboration, connection with Deaf history, and the preservation of American Sign Language.

> *The Garden Wall* by Phyllis Limbacher Tildes (Friends)
>
> *Moses Goes to a Concert* by Isaac Millman (Music and Dance)
>
> *Moses Goes to School* by Isaac Millman (School Days)

**American Sign Language** is the language of the Deaf community of the United States and Canada and is historically related to French Sign Language.

> ASL Deer Mask Craft (Forest Animals)
>
> ASL Friends Magnet Craft (Friends)
>
> *ASL "Handy" Boat Craft (Transportation)
>
> *ASL Tales: Rapunzel* by Judy Hood (Hair)
>
> Caterpillar, Caterpillar (Bugs and Insects)
>
> Community Helpers ASL Matching Game Craft (Community Helpers)
>
> *Cookie Song (Big and Little)
>
> Everybody's Library: A Guessing Game (Books and Libraries)
>
> *Family Song (Family)
>
> *Five Little Flowers (Gardens and Growing)
>
> *Froggy Frolic (Frogs)
>
> *Good Night Song (Bedtime)
>
> *The Handmade Alphabet* by Laura Rankin (Hands)
>
> Hands (Hands)
>
> *Handsigns: A Sign Language Alphabet* by Kathleen Fain (ABC Time)
>
> *I Like Shoes (Shoes)
>
> *"If You're Happy and You Know It" (Feelings)
>
> *In the Forest (Forest Animals)
>
> *"Look at My Hands" (Bath Time)
>
> *Maisy Takes a Bath* by Lucy Cousins (Bath Time)
>
> Marching Around the House (Houses and Homes)
>
> "Mbube" (Jungle Animals)
>
> *Moses Goes to a Concert* by Isaac Millman (Music and Dance)
>
> *Moses Goes to School* by Isaac Millman (School Days)
>
> *My Neighborhood (My Neighborhood)
>
> *The People in My Neighborhood (Community Helpers)
>
> Sibling Song (Brothers and Sisters)
>
> *The Sign for Snow (Winter)
>
> Signing ABCs (ABC Time)
>
> Signing, Signing (Hands)

## DISABILITIES

**DISABILITIES** may be physical, cognitive/mental, sensory, emotional, developmental, or a combination of these. Most people with disabilities prefer a person-first paradigm, in which emphasis is placed on the things a person *can* do.

## EUROPE

**EUROPE** is the world's second-smallest continent.

**Belgium** is known for its gourmet chocolate. In general, Belgians value family, as well as the cleanliness of their homes and public spaces.

**The Czech Republic** is located in central Europe. Its official language is Slovak. Czech culture values humor, egalitarianism, and a down-to-earth mentality.

**Denmark** has a rich Viking history. Danish culture values gender equality and the group over the individual.

**England** is one of four countries that make up the United Kingdom (along with Scotland, Wales, and Northern Ireland). British culture generally values privacy and protocol.

*Finland* is located in northern Europe. Finnish culture values plain speaking.

*My Library Flannelboard (Books and Libraries)

*France* is known for its architecture, cuisine, and wine. French society values privacy and responsibility to family and friends.

*Adele and Simon* by Barbara McClintock (Brothers and Sisters)

"Chez Paris" (Community Helpers)

Crepe Song (Food)

*Crepes by Suzette* by Monica Wellington (Community Helpers)

Fleur-de-Lis Shield Craft (Fairy Tales)

*French* is the second most studied foreign language in the world, after English, and has over 110 million speakers worldwide.

*ABC × 3* Flannelboard (book by Marthe Jocelyn; ABC Time)

*Can You Count Ten Toes? Count to 10 in 10 Different Languages* by Lezlie Evans (Counting)

Everybody's Library: A Guessing Game (Books and Libraries)

Friends Around the World (Friends)

Hands (Hands)

*La Neige Tombe* / Snow Is Falling (Winter)

*Letters Around the World (ABC Time)

Marching Around the House (Houses and Homes)

*Mon Chat Est Beau* (Cats and Dogs)

Name the Color (School Days)

The Old Woman Who Lived in the Shoe (Shoes)

"One Two Three" (Counting)

Parents Around the World (Parents)

*The Perfect Nest* by Catherine Friend (Birds)

To Market All Around the World (Shopping)

What Does Baby Want? Flannelboard (Family)

*The World Turns Round and Round* by Nicki Weiss (Family)

*Germany's* culture generally values planning and thinking ahead, as well as respect for authority.

The Bremen Town Musicians Flannelboard (Music and Dance)

*Dance, Children, Dance! (Music and Dance)

Rapunzel (Hair)

*Sleep, Baby, Sleep! (Parents)

*See also* North America (German American)

*German* is the native language of over 90 million people inside and outside Germany.

Everybody's Library: A Guessing Game (Books and Libraries)

Marching Around the House (Houses and Homes)

"One Two Three" (Counting)

Parents Around the World (Parents)

To Market All Around the World (Shopping)

*Greece* is located in the southern part of Europe. In 776 BC the first Olympic games were held in *Greece*. Modern Greek culture values family, hospitality, and pride in Greek history and culture.

*The Ant and the Grasshopper* by Amy Lowry Poole (Winter)

"Fast and Slow" (Fast and Slow)

*The Hare and the Tortoise* by Helen Ward (Fast and Slow)

**Hungary** is located in Eastern Europe. Family is the center of Hungarian society, with several generations often living together under one roof.

**Ireland** is an island located in the Atlantic Ocean. Eighty-seven percent of the Irish people are Roman Catholic. Irish culture values humor and storytelling.

**Italy** is recognizable for its bootlike shape. Italians are predominantly Roman Catholic. The concept of *bella figure* ("good image") is important to Italians.

**Italian** is an official language of seven countries, including Italy, as well as one of the official languages of the European Union.

**The Netherlands** is located near the North Sea. Dutch society values equality, tolerance of individual differences, attention to detail, and self-control.

**Poland** is located in central Europe. Polish people believe obligation to their family comes first, and often their social and business networks are formed from their family.

**Portugal's** people tend to be very fashion conscious and believe that clothes indicate social standing and success.

**Russia** is the world's biggest country. It encompasses eleven different time zones and spreads across two continents, Europe and Asia.

*"The Clay Pot" (Houses and Homes)

*The Gigantic Turnip* Flannelboard (book by Aleksei Tolstoy; Gardens and Growing)

*How Mama Brought the Spring* by Fran Manushkin (Spring)

May There Always Be Sunshine (Feelings)

*Rechenka's Eggs* by Patricia Polacco (Birds)

Russian Troika (Winter)

*The Snow Child Flannelboard (Winter)

Wish on a Shoe (Shoes)

*"Yasha" Flannelboard (Hair)

**Russian** is the most widely spoken native language in Europe, with over 300 million speakers.

*Can You Count Ten Toes? Count to 10 in 10 Different Languages* by Lezlie Evans (Counting)

"One Two Three" (Counting)

*The World Turns Round and Round* by Nicki Weiss (Family)

**Scotland** is part of the United Kingdom, sharing an island with England. Scottish culture values family ties and a sense of national identity and pride.

Scottish Tartan Weaving Craft (Family)

**Serbia** is located in central/southeastern Europe. Most Serbians are members of the Eastern Orthodox Church.

At the End of the Village (My Neighborhood)

**Slovakia** was part of Czechoslovakia until it gained its independence in 1993. Slovakians are a very private people and often seem reserved upon first meeting.

A Harvest Gift (Fall)

**Spain** is located in southwestern Europe on the Iberian Peninsula. The family is very important in Spanish culture.

"*El Coqui*" (Frogs)

*Un Huevito* / Little Egg (Food)

*See also* North America (Hispanic American)

**Spanish** is the native language of over 329 million people worldwide.

*A la Víbora de la Mar* / Sea Serpent (Under the Sea)

*ABC × 3* Flannelboard (book by Marthe Jocelyn; ABC Time)

Big and Little: A Spanish Game (Big and Little)

*Book Fiesta* by Pat Mora (Books and Libraries)

*¡Bravo!* by Ginger Foglesong Guy (Summer)

Brothers and Sisters Chant (Brothers and Sisters)

*Can You Count Ten Toes? Count to 10 in 10 Different Languages* by Lezlie Evans (Counting)

*Cinco Verde Guisantes* / Five Green Peas (Gardens and Growing)

The Colors of Fall Flannelboard (Fall)

Community Helpers Flannelboard (Community Helpers)

*Count on Culebra* Flannelboard (book by Ann Whitford Paul; Counting)

*Counting Ovejas* by Sarah Weeks (Bedtime)

Down on Grandpa's Farm (Farm Fun)

*El Barrio* by Debbi Chocolate (My Neighborhood)

*El Chocolate* (Food)

"*El Coqui*" (Frogs)

Everybody's Library: A Guessing Game (Books and Libraries)

**Sweden** has a rich Viking history. Swedish culture values humility and egalitarianism.

"*Sma Grodorna* (Sweden)" (Frogs)

*There Was a Little Mouse (Houses and Homes)

**Switzerland** is home to many mountain ranges, including the Alps to the south and the Jura Mountains in the north. Switzerland is known for its neutrality in global conflicts.

Five Saint Bernards (Cats and Dogs)

**How Will We Get to the Beach? A Guessing-Game Story* by Brigitte Luciani (Transportation)

*"Walking Song (Switzerland)" (Transportation)

**Ukraine** is located in Europe and was formerly part of the Soviet Union. Traditional dances are popular and are often performed by both men and women dressed in costume.

*The Little, Little House* by Jessica Souhami (Houses and Homes)

Ukrainian Headdress Festival Wreath Craft (Hair)

Fiji. *See* Oceania

Finland. *See* Europe

France. *See* Europe

French (language). *See* Europe

German (language). *See* Europe

German American. *See* North America

Germany. *See* Europe

Ghana. *See* Africa

Greece. *See* Europe

Haiti. *See* Caribbean

Hawaii. *See* Oceania

Hebrew (language). *See* Middle East

Hindi (language). *See* Asia

Hispanic American. *See* North America

Hungary. *See* Europe

India. *See* Asia

Indonesia. *See* Oceania

Inuit. *See* North America

Iran. *See* Middle East

Iraq. *See* Middle East

Ireland. *See* Europe

Irish American. *See* North America

Israel. *See* Middle East

Italian (language). *See* Europe

Italy. *See* Europe

Jamaica. *See* Caribbean

Japan. *See* Asia

Japanese (language). *See* Asia

Japanese American. *See* North America

Kenya. *See* Africa

Korea. *See* Asia

Korean (language). *See* Asia

## THE MIDDLE EAST is a region that includes West Asia and North Africa.

> *The Golden Sandal* by Rebecca Hickox (Shoes)
>
> How Do We Get Around? (Transportation)
>
> *How Many Donkeys? An Arabic Counting Tale* by Margaret Read MacDonald and Nadia Jameel Taibah (Counting)
>
> *\*The World Turns Round and Round* by Nicki Weiss (Family)

**Egypt** is located in northern Africa and is known for its rich history and its location on the Nile River. Egyptian culture values family, honor, and hospitality.

> *The Egyptian Cinderella* by Shirley Climo (Fairy Tales)
>
> Papyrus Craft (Books and Libraries)
>
> *Temple Cat* by Andrew Clements (Cats and Dogs)
>
> *What's the Matter, Habibi?* by Betsy Lewin (Hats)

**Iran** was known as Persia until 1935. Iranian culture puts loyalty to the family before every other relationship.

> "The Pumpkin Child" Flannelboard (Fall)

**Iraq** was formerly known as Mesopotamia, and its official language is Arabic. Iraqi culture values family, honor, and hospitality.

> *The Golden Sandal* by Rebecca Hickox (Shoes)
>
> *The Librarian of Basra: A True Story from Iraq* by Jeanette Winter (Books and Libraries)

**Israel** was officially formed in 1948, when Palestine was partitioned for its creation. This land in the Middle East was part of an area known as Canaan, which the Jewish Torah said was to be given to the Jewish people.

> *The Little, Little House* by Jessica Souhami (Houses and Homes)
>
> The Magic Pomegranate Flannelboard (Fairy Tales)
>
> "*Mi Jachol Lassim* (Israel)" (Friends)
>
> \*Something Out of Nothing Flannelboard (Clothes)
>
> "*Tu-tu-tu-tu*" (Nature)

**Hebrew** is the language of the Jewish people.

> *Can You Count Ten Toes? Count to 10 in 10 Different Languages* by Lezlie Evans (Counting)
>
> Hello (Friends)
>
> "*Rosh, Ktefayim, Birkayim, Etzba'ot* / Head, Shoulders, Knees, and Toes" (My Body)

**Lebanon** is a small, mountainous country. Football is the most popular sport in Lebanon, and the country has a long tradition of music and arts.

> My Boat Is Going (Transportation)

**Palestine** is located within certain regions of Israel, most notably the Gaza Strip. Extended families tend to live together in one house, with many generations together including married children and grandparents.

> The Little Pot Flannelboard (Shopping)

***Turkey*** was once part of the Ottoman Empire. Turkish culture tends to value relationships over competition.

> *Nabeel's New Pants: An Eid Tale* by Fawzia Gilani-Williams (Clothes)
>
> Splish, Splash, Splish! (Bath Time)

Mongolia. *See* Asia

Morocco. *See* Africa

Myanmar. *See* Asia

Native American. *See* North America

Netherlands. *See* Europe

New Zealand. *See* Oceania

Nicaragua. *See* Central America

Nigeria. *See* Africa

# NORTH AMERICA is the third-largest continent in area and the fourth-largest in population.

***African American*** is a term used to describe any citizens or residents of the United States who have origins in the black populations of Africa.

> *Aunt Flossie's Hats (and Crab Cakes Later)* by Elizabeth Fitzgerald Howard (Hats)
>
> *Drumbeat in Our Feet* by Patricia A. Keeler (Music and Dance)
>
> *Happy to Be Nappy* by bell hooks (Hair)
>
> How Frog Got Eyes and Mole Got a Tail Flannelboard (Frogs)
>
> *Jonathan and His Mommy* by Irene Smalls (My Neighborhood)
>
> *Leola and the Honeybears* Flannelboard (book by Melodye Benson Rosales; Big and Little)
>
> *Leola and the Honeybears* Stick Puppets (Big and Little)
>
> Peep Squirrel (Fall)
>
> *Shante Keys and the New Year's Peas* by Gail Piernas-Davenport (Holidays and Celebrations)
>
> *The Wide-Mouthed Frog* by Keith Faulkner (Frogs)

The ***American Southwest*** includes the areas between California and Texas, and its culture incorporates many Hispanic and Native American influences.

> *Cactus Hotel* by Brenda Guiberson (Summer)
>
> *So Happy!* by Kevin Henkes (Feelings)

***Appalachia*** is a term used to describe a cultural region in the eastern United States that stretches from New York to northern Alabama, Mississippi, and Georgia.

> *That Book Woman* by Heather Henson (Books and Libraries)

***Canada*** is divided into provinces and territories. Many Canadians have British, French, or Native American ancestors. Canadian culture values the individual's responsibility to the community.

> *La Neige Tombe / Snow Is Falling* (Winter)

***Chinese American*** is a term for Chinese immigrants or those of Chinese descent who live in the United States.

> *Brothers* by Yin (Brothers and Sisters)
>
> *Lissy's Friends* by Grace Lin (Friends)
>
> *The Ugly Vegetables* by Grace Lin (Gardens and Growing)

***German American*** is a term for German immigrants or those of German descent who live in the United States.

> *When I First Came to This Land* Flannelboard (book by Harriet Ziefert; Farm Fun)

**Hispanic American** is a term for Latino immigrants or those of Latino descent who live in the United States.

> *ABC Rhyme Time (ABC Time)
>
> *Carlos and the Squash Plant Flannelboard (Bath Time)
>
> *El Barrio by Debbi Chocolate (My Neighborhood)
>
> El Chocolate (Food)
>
> *Kitchen Dance by Maurie J. Manning (Music and Dance)
>
> *Papá and Me by Arthur Dorros (Parents)
>
> *Siesta (Bedtime)
>
> *Siesta Flannelboard (book by Ginger Foglesong Guy; Bedtime)
>
> *The Three Little Tamales by Eric A. Kimmel (Fairy Tales)

The **Inuit** are the native people of northern Canada. The Inuit continue to use their traditional language, hunt for food, and make wood and bone carvings.

> Mama, Do You Love Me? Flannelboard (book by Barbara M. Joosse; Parents)
>
> *Nanook and Pryce by Ned Crowley (Under the Sea)
>
> *On Mother's Lap by Ann Herbert Scott (Parents)
>
> *The Three Snow Bears by Jan Brett (Winter)

**Irish American** is a term for Irish immigrants or those of Irish descent who live in the United States.

> Brothers by Yin (Brothers and Sisters)

**Japanese American** is a term for Japanese immigrants or those of Japanese descent who live in the United States.

> Butterflies for Kiri by Cathryn Falwell (Spring)
>
> Yoko by Rosemary Wells (Food)
>
> Yoko Writes Her Name by Rosemary Wells (School Days)
>
> Yoko's Paper Cranes by Rosemary Wells (Family)

**Mexico** is located between the United States and Central America. Mexican society values the family and is generally hierarchical.

> A la Víbora de la Mar / Sea Serpent (Under the Sea)
>
> *Book Fiesta by Pat Mora (Books and Libraries)
>
> Borreguita and the Coyote Flannelboard (book by Verna Aardema; Farm Fun)
>
> Erandi's Braids by Antonio Hernandez Madrigal (Hair)
>
> The Fisherman and the Turtle by Eric A. Kimmel (Under the Sea)
>
> Huichol Yarn Painting Craft (My Neighborhood)
>
> Just a Minute Flannelboard (book by Yuyi Morales; Counting)
>
> "Mexican Handclapping Song" (Hands)
>
> "Mexican Hat Dance" (Hats; Music and Dance)
>
> Monarch Butterfly Craft (Bugs and Insects)
>
> Native Mexican Baskets Craft (Shopping)
>
> Numero Uno by Alex Dorros and Arthur Dorros (Feelings)
>
> Papel Picado Craft (Holidays and Celebrations)
>
> Rain Player by David Wisniewski (Weather)
>
> *What Can You Do with a Rebozo? by Carmen Tafolla (Clothes)
>
> See also North America (Hispanic American); Europe (Spanish [language])

**Native American** refers to any of the native peoples of North America.

    Berry Ink Craft (School Days)

    *Boat Ride with Lillian Two Blossom* by Patricia Polacco (Weather)

    Coyote Steals the Spring Flannelboard (Spring)

    Dreamcatcher Craft (Bedtime)

    *Giving Thanks: A Native American Good Morning Message* by Chief Jake Swamp (Nature)

    The Gossiping Clams Flannelboard (Under the Sea)

    Grandmother Spider Brings the Light Flannelboard (Weather)

    Huckleberry Harvest Flannelboard (Summer)

    *Jingle Dancer* by Cynthia Leitich Smith (Music and Dance)

    *The Legend of the Lady Slipper* by Lise Lunge-Larsen and Margi Preus (Shoes)

    *Mole's Hill* by Lois Ehlert (Forest Animals)

    Native American Painting Craft (Nature)

    Native American Tepee Craft (Houses and Homes)

    *"Ride, Horse, Ride" (Farm Fun)

    *Snowshoes, Snowshoes (Winter)

    *The Sun's Daughter* by Pat Sherman (Winter)

    *Thanks to the Animals* by Allen Sockabasin (Forest Animals)

    *Turtle's Race with Beaver* by Joseph Bruchac (Fast and Slow)

    *Turtle's Race with Beaver* Puppets Craft (Fast and Slow)

    Why Opossum Has a Bare Tail Flannelboard (Forest Animals)

    Zuni Harvest Dance (Music and Dance)

    *See also* North America (Inuit)

**Pakistani American** refers to Pakistani immigrants or those of Pakistani descent who live in the United States.

    *Nadia's Hands* by Karen English (Hands)

**See also** Oceania (Hawaii); Caribbean (Puerto Rico)

# OCEANIA is a region that includes the islands of the South Pacific Ocean.

**Fiji** is an island nation whose culture combines elements of indigenous, Indian, Chinese, and European traditions.

    *The Butterfly and the Crane Prop Story (Fast and Slow)

**Hawaii,** which is part of the United States, consists of seven islands in the Pacific Ocean. Modern Hawaii blends people from Japanese, South Pacific, and western backgrounds with those of Hawaiian ancestry. Traditional Hawaiian culture values sympathy, kindness, unpretentiousness, and harmony.

    Aloha Song (Holidays and Celebrations)

    Hawaiian Lei Craft (Spring)

    Hello Hands (Hands)

    *Hula Lullaby* by Erin Eitter Kono (Bedtime)

    *Ke Ao Nani* / This Beautiful World (Nature)

    *Luka's Quilt* by Georgia Guback (Family)

**Indonesia** consists of over seventeen thousand islands scattered between Asia and Australia. With over three hundred different ethnic groups, it has an extremely diverse culture.

    Desaku, My Village (My Neighborhood)

    "One Two Three" (Counting)

**The Marshall Islands** are located between Hawaii and Australia in the Pacific Ocean. People on the Marshall Islands live together in "cookhouse groups" of extended family.

Surf War! by Margaret Read MacDonald (Under the Sea)

**New Zealand** is an island southeast of Australia. Eighty percent of New Zealanders are of European descent (*Pakeha*), with 20 percent of Maori and Pacific Islander background. New Zealand's culture generally values hospitality and shuns traditional class structures.

In the Country of New Zealand (School Days)

Pakistan. *See* Asia
Pakistani American. *See* North America
Palestine. *See* Middle East
Panama. *See* Central America
Peru. *See* South America
Philippines. *See* Asia
Poland. *See* Europe
Portugal. *See* Europe
Puerto Rico. *See* Caribbean

Russia. *See* Europe
Russian (language). *See* Europe

Scotland. *See* Europe
Serbia. *See* Europe
Singapore. *See* Asia
Slovakia. *See* Europe
South Africa. *See* Africa

# SOUTH AMERICA is a continent made up of twelve independent nations.

*Buzz Buzz Buzz by Verónica Uribe (Bugs and Insects)
The Great Kapok Tree by Lynne Cherry (Nature)
In the South American Rain Forest (Fast and Slow)
*Market Day by Lois Ehlert (Shopping)
Poison Dart Frog Puppet Craft (Frogs)
*"Slowly, Slowly, Slowly," Said the Sloth by Eric Carle (Fast and Slow)

**Brazil** is the biggest country in South America and contains much of the Amazon rain forest. Its people come from a variety of backgrounds, but almost all of them speak Portuguese.

Dress Up (Clothes)
How Beetle Got Her Beautiful Coat Flannelboard (Bugs and Insects)
*My Hat Has Three Corners (Hats)
*So Say the Little Monkeys by Nancy Van Laan (Jungle Animals)

**Chile** is located on the western and southwestern coast of South America. The family and the Roman Catholic Church play important parts in Chile's culture.

*The Farmyard Jamboree by Margaret Read MacDonald (Farm Fun)

**Colombia** is located in the northern region of South America. The family and the Roman Catholic Church play important parts in Colombia's culture.

*Biblioburro: A True Story from Colombia by Jeanette Winter (Books and Libraries)
The Kite Festival by Leyla Torres (Spring)
Paper *Mola* Garden Craft (Gardens and Growing)

***Ecuador*** was once part of the Inca empire. The population of Ecuador is a mix of Mestizo (mixed Native American and white), Native American, Spanish, and African, as well as more than fourteen indigenous groups.

>  *\*Papito, Mamita* (Parents)

***Peru*** was once home to the Incas, who constructed ten thousand miles of roads, bridges, aqueducts, mountain temples, and palaces. Modern Peruvian culture, language, and music mix traditional values with Spanish influences.

>  *Carolina's Gift: A Story of Peru* by Katacha Diaz (Family)
>
>  *Chaleco*: A Guessing Rhyme (Clothes)
>
>  Peruvian *Chaleco* Craft (Clothes)

Spain. *See* Europe

Spanish (language). *See* Europe

Sri Lanka. *See* Asia

Swahili (language). *See* Africa

Sweden. *See* Europe

Switzerland. *See* Europe

Tagalog (language). *See* Asia

Thailand. *See* Asia

Tibet. *See* Asia

Trinidad and Tobago. *See* Caribbean

Turkey. *See* Middle East

Uganda. *See* Africa

Ukraine. *See* Europe

Vietnam. *See* Asia

Vietnamese (language). *See* Asia

Zambia. *See* Africa

Zanzibar. *See* Africa

Zimbabwe. *See* Africa

Zulu. *See* Africa

# Entries Incorporating Multiple Cultures

*The Autumn Equinox: Celebrating the Harvest* by Ellen Jackson (Fall)

*Be My Neighbor* by Maya Ajmera and John D. Ivanko (My Neighborhood)

*Birthday Customs Around the World* by Sarah L. Schuette (Holidays and Celebrations)

*\*Bread Bread Bread* by Ann Morris (Food)

*Can You Count Ten Toes? Count to 10 in 10 Different Languages* by Lezlie Evans (Counting)

"Circle of Friends" (Friends)

Create a Mixed-Up Fairy Tale (Fairy Tales)

Dress Up (Clothes)

Friends Around the World (Friends)

*Glass Slipper, Gold Sandal: A Worldwide Cinderella* by Paul Fleischman (Fairy Tales)

Going to the Market (Shopping)

# APPENDIX B

# Storytime Materials Celebrating Diversity

Materials especially appropriate for toddler storytimes are starred.

## Books

Ajmera, Maya, and John D. Ivanko. *Animal Friends: A Global Celebration of Children and Animals*. Watertown, MA: Charlesbridge, 2002.
> Full-color illustrations and simple text show pets around the world.

———. *To Be a Kid*. Watertown, MA: Charlesbridge, 2004.
> Full-color illustrations and simple text celebrate the experience of being a kid all around the world.

Barnwell, Ysaye. *We Are One*. New York: Harcourt, 1993.
> A lyrical celebration of our similarities, regardless of country or race.

Beeler, Selby B. *Throw Your Tooth on the Roof: Tooth Traditions from Around the World*. Boston: Houghton Mifflin, 1998.
> This winsomely illustrated book explores tooth traditions from around the world. While the book is too long to read in its entirety in storytime, the geographical grouping and short descriptions of traditions in each country make it easy to pick a few items to share in a program.

Casely, Judith. *Harry and Willy and Carrothead*. New York: Greenwillow, 1991.
> Harry was born with no left hand. Oscar was born with red hair. They soon figure out that appearances don't matter a bit when it comes to being friends.

Cooper, Floyd. *Cumbayah*. New York: Morrow, 1998.
> This adaptation of the traditional gospel folk tune, from Gullah roots, has universal applications as it depicts people from cultures all over the world and their similarities—they all hurt, laugh, cry, and need help.

Cooper, Ilene. *The Golden Rule*. New York: Abrams, 2007.
> A boy and his grandfather discover the various iterations of the Golden Rule in cultures around the world.

English, Karen. *Speak English for Us, Marisol!* Morton Grove, IL: Whitman, 2000.
> Though Marisol may grow tired of helping her family communicate in English, she knows they appreciate her help.

Evans, Lezlie. *Can You Greet the Whole Wide World? Twelve Common Phrases in Twelve Different Languages*. Boston: Houghton Mifflin, 2006.
> A simple story of a school day introduces phrases such as "good morning," "what's your name?" and "thank you" in twelve world languages.

*Fox, Mem. *Ten Little Fingers and Ten Little Toes*. New York: Houghton Mifflin, 2008.
With charming illustrations by Helen Oxenbury, this lovely little book celebrates babies around the world.

———. *Whoever You Are*. New York: Harcourt, 1997.
This beautifully illustrated book celebrates the diversity of children around the world and the similarities in feelings, friendship, and love.

Gilchrist, Jan Spivey. *My America*. New York: HarperCollins, 2007.
This picture book poem celebrates the diversity of America.

*Global Fund for Children. *Global Babies*. Watertown, MA: Charlesbridge, 2009.
This photo-illustrated board book presents a beautiful message that emphasizes how babies around the world are all loved and special, even as it showcases their diversity.

Gray, Nigel. *A Country Far Away*. New York: Orchard, 1988.
A boy in Africa and a boy in America tell about their daily lives. The text emphasizes their commonalities while the illustrations show the different ways that they attend school, help their parents, and play with friends.

Hamanaka, Sheila. *All the Colors of the Earth*. New York: Morrow, 1995.
Lyrical text and striking oil paintings celebrate the diversity of children around the world.

Isadora, Rachel. *Say Hello!* New York: Putnam, 2010.
A girl and her dog walk down the street saying hello in many different languages to all the people that they meet.

Katz, Karen. *Can You Say Peace?* New York: Henry Holt, 2006.
In bright, vibrant illustrations, children around the world introduce different ways to say *peace*.

———. *The Colors of Us*. New York: Henry Holt: 1999.
Lena and her mother, an artist, explore the many beautiful shades in the skin of their friends and family.

Kerley, Barbara. *A Little Peace*. Washington, DC: National Geographic, 2007.
With stunning photos from around the world, this book shares a message of peace between individuals, families, and nations.

———. *One World, One Day*. Washington, DC: National Geographic, 2009.
Gorgeous photos of children around the world join with a simple text that emphasizes the similarities in the lives of all children.

Kitze, Carrie A. *I Don't Have Your Eyes*. Warren, NJ: EMK Press, 2003.
In this gentle exploration of similarities and differences, children forge connections with their caregivers even if they don't look alike.

*Miller, J. Philip, and Sheppard M. Greene. *We All Sing with the Same Voice*. New York: HarperCollins, 2001.
Rhyming text and colorful illustrations celebrate all types of diversity. The text is from a song originally heard on television's *Sesame Street*.

Mora, Pat. *Join Hands! The Ways We Celebrate Life*. Watertown, MA: Charlesbridge, 2008.
Rhyming text and colorful photos by George Ancona explore celebrations around the world.

Park, Linda Sue, and Julie Durango. *Yum! Yuck! A Foldout Book of People Sounds*. Watertown, MA: Charlesbridge, 2005.
Each double-page spread features vocabulary from a variety of countries, with illustrations inviting readers to guess the meaning. When the page is folded out, the English translation is revealed. This book focuses on simple, universal concepts, such as "Yikes!" "Ah-choo!" and "Wow!"

*Pinkney, Sandra L. *A Rainbow All Around Me*. New York: Scholastic, 2002.
A multiethnic cast of kids celebrates the colors of the rainbow.

Pollak, Barbara. *Our Community Garden*. Hillsboro, OR: Beyond Words, 2004.
    A group of friends in San Francisco plants vegetables in their community garden that reflect their varied heritages and celebrate their harvest with salsa, stir-fry, eggplant stew, potato pie, and carrot cake.

Ruurs, Margriet. *My School in the Rain Forest*. Honesdale, PA: Boyds Mills Press, 2009.
    This book explores various types of schools found around the world.

Shirley, Debra. *Best Friend on Wheels*. Morton Grove, IL: Whitman, 2008.
    A little girl tells about her best friend, Sarah, who happens to use a wheelchair. When she first met Sarah, she "only saw the wheelchair," but now she sees Sarah and what a great person she is.

Stojic, Manya. *Hello World! Greetings in Forty-two Languages Around the Globe!* New York: Scholastic, 2002.
    Bright, bold pictures accompany information about greetings in many languages, along with phonetic pronunciations.

Thomas, Shelley Moore. *Somewhere Today: A Book of Peace*. Morton Grove, IL: Whitman, 1998.
    Accompanied by photos of diverse children around the world, this book explores simple ways that anyone can make the world a better place.

Thong, Roseanne. *Wish: Wishing Traditions Around the World*. San Francisco: Chronicle, 2008.
    A nonfiction exploration of wishing traditions from around the world. Though the book is too long to share in storytime, the organization makes it easy to pick a few to share.

Tyler, Michael. *The Skin You Live In*. Chicago, IL: Chicago Children's Museum, 2005.
    A rhyming celebration of skin of every color.

*Walsh, Melanie. *My Nose, Your Nose*. New York: Houghton Mifflin, 2002.
    Children from around the world discover how they are different, yet have much in common.

Weiss, George David, and Bob Thiele. *What a Wonderful World*. New York: Simon and Schuster, 1995.
    Bright, bold illustrations by Ashley Bryan accompany the text of the classic song performed by the great Louis Armstrong. Featuring children of various races performing a puppet show, this book is a moving tribute to the simple, powerful lyrics. Rather than reading, try playing a recording of the song as you share the pictures.

Williams, Sam. *Talk Peace*. New York: Holiday House, 2005.
    Sunny illustrations and simple text call on all the people of the world to "talk peace."

# Music

Barchas, Sarah. *Bridges Across the World: A Multicultural Songfest*. Sonoita, AZ: High Haven Music, 1999.
    This CD features thirty songs from around the world, all appropriate for use in storytime. The accompanying book contains lyrics and language notes.

*Beall, Pamela Conn, and Susan Hagen Nipp. *Wee Sing Around the World*. New York: Price Stern Sloan, 1998.
    Simple fingerplays and rhymes from around the world.

Buchman, Rachel. *Jewish Holiday Songs for Children*. Cambridge, MA: Rounder, 1993.
    Songs in Hebrew and English celebrate Jewish holidays throughout the year.

Daria. *Beautiful Rainbow World*. Riegelsville, PA: DariaMusic, 2007.
    Songstress Daria shares songs celebrating the diversity of the world.

*I Will Be Your Friend: Songs and Activities for Young Peacemakers.* Montgomery, AL: Southern
  Poverty Law Center, 2003.
  Songs, lyrics, and activities to teach about tolerance.

Jenkins, Ella. *Multicultural Children's Songs.* Washington, DC: Smithsonian Folkways, 1995.
  Songs for children from many traditions.

——. *Sharing Cultures with Ella Jenkins.* Washington, DC: Smithsonian Folkways, 2003.
  Ella Jenkins takes children on a trip around the world through music.

Jordan, Sara. *Celebrate the Human Race: Multicultural Songs and Activities for Children.* Niagara
  Falls, NY: Jordan Music Productions, 1993.
  This CD with accompanying booklet features songs from many lands, with instructions and
  activities for using them with groups of children.

Mattox, Cheryl Warren. *Shake It to the One That You Love the Best: Play Songs and Lullabies from
  Black Musical Traditions.* El Sobrante, CA: Warren-Mattox Productions, 1989.
  This CD with accompanying booklet features songs, games, and rhymes from the African
  American tradition.

Orozco, Jose-Luis. *De Colores and Other Latin American Folk Songs for Children.* Berkeley, CA:
  Arcoiris Records, 1996.
  Simple songs for children in Spanish, perfect for storytime. A book by the same title (New
  York: Dutton, 1994) is also available, which features complete sheet music and lyrics for the
  songs on the CD.

*Rhythm 4 Kids: World Sing-a-long.* Franklin, TN: Naxos of America, 2004.
  A variety of songs from around the world.

Skiera-Zucak, Lois. *Songs About Native Americans.* Long Branch, NJ: Kimbo Educational, 1994.
  Original and traditional songs celebrate Native American traditions.

Sol y Canto. *El Doble de Amigos / Twice as Many Friends.* Cambridge, MA: Rounder Kids, 2003.
  This bilingual English/Spanish CD provides wonderful dancing music.

Stewart, Georgiana. *Children's Folk Dances.* Long Branch, NJ: Kimbo Educational, 1998.
  This lively CD contains folk songs from around the world, along with instructions for using
  them with groups of children.

*——. *Multicultural Bean Bag Fun.* Long Branch, NJ: Kimbo Educational, 2009.
  Beanbag activities set to music around the world, each designed for groups.

# APPENDIX C

# Further Resources for Storytime Planning

Braman, Arlette N. *Kids Around the World Create!* New York: Wiley, 1999.

Carlson, Ann, and Mary Carlson. *Flannelboard Stories for Infants and Toddlers, Bilingual Edition.* Chicago: American Library Association, 2005.

DeSpain, Pleasant. *Thirty-three Multicultural Tales to Tell.* Little Rock, AR: August House, 1993.

Esche, Maria Bonfanti, and Clare Bonfanti Braham. *Kids Celebrate! Activities for Special Days Throughout the Year.* Chicago: Chicago Review Press, 1998.

Gould, Roberta. *The Kids' Multicultural Craft Book.* Charlotte, VT: Williamson, 2004.

Hamilton, Leslie. *Child's Play Around the World: 170 Crafts, Games, and Projects for Two-to-Six-Year-Olds.* New York: Perigee, 1996.

Harrington, Janice N. *Multiculturalism in Library Programming for Children.* Chicago: American Library Association, 1994.

Hart, Avery, and Paul Mantell. *Kids Make Music!* Charlotte, VT: Williamson, 1993.

Holt, David, and Bill Mooney, eds. *More Ready-to-Tell Tales from Around the World.* Little Rock, AR: August House, 2007.

Jefferies, David. *Multicultural Folk Tales.* Westminster, CA: Teacher Created Materials, 1992.

Kalman, Bobbie. *Multicultural Meals.* New York: Crabtree, 2003.

Kuharets, Olga, ed. *Venture into Cultures: A Resource Book of Multicultural Materials and Programs.* Chicago: American Library Association, 2001.

MacDonald, Margaret Read. *Celebrate the World: Twenty Tellable Folktales for Multicultural Festivals.* New York: H. W. Wilson, 1994.

MacMillan, Kathy. *Try Your Hand at This! Easy Ways to Incorporate Sign Language into Your Programs.* Lanham, MD: Scarecrow Press, 2005.

MacMillan, Kathy, and Christine Kirker. *Kindergarten Magic: Theme-Based Lessons for Building Literacy and Library Skills.* Chicago: American Library Association, 2012.

——. *Storytime Magic: 400 Fingerplays, Flannelboards, and Other Activities.* Chicago: American Library Association, 2009.

Milord, Susan. *Hands Around the World: 365 Creative Ways to Build Cultural Awareness and Global Respect.* Charlotte, VT: Williamson, 1992.

——. *Tales Alive! Ten Multicultural Folktales with Activities.* Charlotte, VT: Williamson, 1995.

Pollock, Jean M. *Side by Side: Twelve Multicultural Puppet Plays.* Lanham, MD: Scarecrow Press, 1998.

Press, Judy. *Around the World Art and Activities.* Charlotte, VT: Williamson, 2001.

Sierra, Judy. *Multicultural Folktales for the Feltboard and Readers' Theater.* Phoenix, AZ: Oryx, 1996.

Trevino, Rose Zertuche. *Read Me a Rhyme in Spanish and English.* Chicago: American Library Association, 2009.

Webber, Desiree, Dee Ann Corn, Elaine Harrod, Donna Norvell, and Sandy Shropshire. *Travel the Globe: Multicultural Story Times.* Englewood, CO: Libraries Unlimited, 1998.

# Index of Names and Titles